A DIFFERENT WORLD

My Life
and
Making a Difference
in the World

Margaret Krug Palen

HERITAGE BOOKS
2018

HERITAGE BOOKS
AN IMPRINT OF HERITAGE BOOKS, INC.

Books, CDs, and more—Worldwide

For our listing of thousands of titles see our website at
www.HeritageBooks.com

Published 2018 by
HERITAGE BOOKS, INC.
Publishing Division
5810 Ruatan Street
Berwyn Heights, Md. 20740

Copyright © 2018 Margaret Krug Palen

Heritage Books by the author:
A Different World: My Life and Making a Difference in the World
Genealogical Guide to Tracing Ancestors in Germany
Genealogical Research Guide to Germany
German Settlers of Iowa: Their Descendants and European Ancestors
German Settlers of Iowa: Their Descendants and European Ancestors, Revised Edition

All rights reserved. No part of this book may be reproduced or transmitted in any form or by any means, electronic or mechanical, including photocopying, recording or by any information storage and retrieval system without written permission from the author, except for the inclusion of brief quotations in a review.

International Standard Book Number
Paperbound: 978-0-7884-5835-4

A Different World

Top row: Grandmother Susan Palen Mc Hugh
Bottom row: Granddaughter Andrea McHugh Campbell
holding Great-Granddaughter Avery Campbell,
Great-Grandmother Margaret Krug Palen.

Margaret Krug Palen

A Different World

TABLE OF CONTENTS

INTRODUCTION	vii
CHAPTER 1 - *20th Century America*	9
CHAPTER 2 - *Siblings*	17
CHAPTER 3 - *Education*	23
CHAPTER 4 - *Farm Years*	43
CHAPTER 5 - *Employment*	55
CHAPTER 6 – *Marriage*	65
CHAPTER 7 - *Palen's Pacific Perch*	77
CHAPTER 8 - *Oregon's Capital City*	85
CHAPTER 9 - *This Changing World*	113
CHAPTER 10 - *Europe and Change in China*	129
CHAPTER 11 – *Scotland, Ireland and Retirement*	141
CHAPTER 12 - *The Holy Land and Egypt*	163

CHAPTER 13 - *American Making a Difference*   173

CHAPTER 14 - *Mozambique, Africa*   197

CHAPTER 15 - *Belarus, Europe Project*   209

CHAPTER 16 - *Bolivia, South America*   219

CHAPTER 17 - *Jamaica, West Indies*   231

CHAPTER 18 - *Epilogue*   243

INTRODUCTION

As time is the most valuable thing that I have, because it is the most irrevocable, and I want to preserve the experiences in my lifetime, I write this account of them. I cannot write about the events and happenings without a constant sense of gratitude for my American life and my desire to make a difference in this changing world.

At my age, I can continue my quest to make a difference in everything I do; though getting older, I still praise the Lord for his constant presence in my life through the Holy Spirit. I attend church and go to organization meetings. The simple joys in life are the secret to longevity.

A cousin corresponding with me about family genealogy wrote: "For a little Iowa girl you have really gone a long way and made something of yourself. I admire you for all you have done and continue to do."

Margaret Krug Palen

CHAPTER 1
20th Century America

"Here a little, and there a little." - Isaiah 28:10 describes memories of my early days in the 20th century. It makes little difference how old I am, or what I have experienced; there are times in my life that affect me so deeply that no matter what I do, no matter how hard I try to erase them, my mind will never let those memories fade.

Herbert Hoover was the 31st president of our country when I was born. His birth home and early years were twenty miles "as the crow flies" from the farm home where I was born. Years later, I lived in the same city in Oregon where Herbert Hoover lived in years of his youth. The coinage of my birth year was buffalo nickels and Indian head pennies, so common in my youth they were given to me for money to buy penny candies and a five cent ice cream cone.

I am the first generation of my German family in America to speak English as a first language. My family in Europe lived in a farming village in the middle of Germany, and their home in America became prairie farms in the middle of the country. My German grandparents both descended from the same village in Germany. My father's Teutonic characteristics were obvious in his blond hair, blue eyes, fair complexion, and six foot stature with German his first language.

My birth was in the first floor bedroom of a farm house owned by my German grandparents. My grandparents owned all the farms their four sons lived on, making them large landowners in the community. I was named after my maternal great grandfather and his mother Margaret Lovaire. Great Grandpa raised my mother, and was an immigrant from Alsace Lorraine in German northeast France.

There was no running water in our farm home, and there was an outhouse in the backyard. Saturday night baths were taken in a tub placed on the kitchen floor. My early year memories are of family meals around the kitchen table. The only time I saw my father during the farming years was at evening meals, usually around 6 p.m., or after the dairy herd was milked and all evening farm chores completed. Summer and autumn months, father helped his three brothers with their crops that included eating meals with them.

My seat at mealtime in our home was on the west side of the walnut table that was also the only kitchen work area. My parents ate breakfast at that table early every morning after father finished milking, separating cream from the milk, and had finished all farm chores before the children were awake. The east side of the table was where my two sisters sat and they faced me. Mother's seat at meals was on the north side of the table, the south side is where father sat. The bench I sat on was constructed by father to serve also for butchering and sausage making; for meals it was placed up against the radio console between the two windows on the west side of the kitchen. When father wanted to hear market reports during a meal, he asked me to turn on the radio or to turn up the volume since I was nearest the radio. I could easily reach around behind my back to perform the task.

A memorable meal, when the radio was turned on low and faintly heard, was Sunday, December 7, 1941, when father asked me to quickly turn up the volume. I responded to increase the sound and we heard the news of the bombing of Pearl Harbor.

"We're in war!" father exclaimed.

A Different World

"What is war?" I asked. I cannot remember all that my parents said, but they began recalling World War I that occurred in their youth, and it amazed me that they had lived through a war though it was somewhat a comfort to realize it at that time.

Not long after World War II in Europe ended, and I had walked home from school, I heard an interrupting radio news bulletin about President Roosevelt's death. I could not remember a time when he was not president because he had been in office so many years of my life. I ran to the barnyard to find my father and tell him about the president's death.

Weeks later, after the dropping of the atomic bomb on Japan, my German grandpa was working on our farm; August 14—the day news about the end of the war in the Pacific was expected. Grandpa decided to drive to the city for dinner that evening and he told my mother about what time he would leave our farm.

"Can I ride with Grandpa and stay all night with Grandma?" I inquired. My maternal grandmother lived in the city. Mother gave me permission to ride with Grandpa and he dropped me off at my maternal grandma's house. She greeted me with news just coming over the radio; the official announcement that World War II in the Pacific had come to an end.

"There will be a big celebration downtown," Grandma said to me.

I telephoned my favorite first cousin that lived within walking distance of both Grandma and the bridges across the river into the downtown area of the city. We immediately met and walked across the bridges into the downtown area that was completely jammed with people out on all of the streets. People left the downtown businesses when they heard the news the war was over and they went immediately out into the streets to rejoice. The crush of people milling about hugging each other, ecstatic about the news; I will never forget it or expect to ever see it again. There were so many people we could only move when the crowd moved. That expression of happiness was overwhelming!

Talk around my family's meal table in my youth often centered on my parent's memories. Mother recalled the fire of 1916 that burned down the main street of the town of Newhall where she lived with her grandparents in her youth. She remembered that she ran downtown to watch, and her grandmother went to the Wagner-Roberts store to carry out bolts of dry goods, but they were too heavy and she had to quit. This memory always brought up the Great Chicago Fire. Mother's relatives lived in Illinois and when they were in our farm home their memories often recalled the fire that broke out when a cow owned by Mrs. O'Leary kicked over a lighted lantern in a barn. Fanned by strong winds, 17,450 buildings were destroyed in an area of three and one-third square miles. The flames killed at least 300 persons, left 390,000 homeless, and destroyed $200,000,000 worth of property. Perhaps talk about my father's barn and cows, and the lanterns he used in the barn stirred up the family to talk about the Chicago fire.

I learned about the German culture of my father's family at mealtimes. Mother was raised by her Scottish grandmother and sometimes had different viewpoints; however, father prevailed with his male dominant German culture. Mother laughingly explained Germans and Scots married because they had the same values, though sometimes they were in reverse order! Mother's Scottish thrift always fit in with father's plans. There was never anything wasted in the kitchen. The dog or the hogs on our farm ate every unused scrap of food.

Mother prepared only one chicken for a meal, and everyone knew which piece was the favorite of each family member and that made it possible for each person to eat their preferred piece of chicken. Mother butchered a chicken by scalding the feet, peeling them, and frying them along with other chicken pieces. My older sister and I each ate a chicken foot and a chicken leg. Mother and my younger sister each ate a wing. Father preferred the chicken breast. When my German grandpa ate meals with us he wanted to eat the back of the chicken.

After my German grandmother's death, Grandpa lived with us in the years when he built smaller buildings on the farm, and when the large elevator corn-crib was under construction.

Sometimes mother choked on her food and father requested she leave the table and return when she had recovered. I never forgot it because it happened often enough that it always remained in my memory. In my fiftieth year I was diagnosed with a hiatus hernia in my first upper GI and lower GI physical examination, though I had no symptoms of it. My doctor asked if anyone in my family had choking problems. I instantly recalled my mother's choking. The doctor explained hiatus hernias are inherited and can be traced in family lines. Then I learned both of my sisters had a hernia diagnosed at a younger age. Fortunately, my doctor warned me not to eat or drink anything with caffeine in it, and not to drink red wine, however, I could drink white wine and champagne.

A very short distance north of our farm home was the location of the Chicago, Milwaukee, St. Paul and Pacific Railroads roundhouse, ten side tracks, a turntable and stalls for locomotives, a power house, restaurant, bunkhouse, coal and ice station tipple. Ice from the Great Lakes was stored and used in the steam engines. The freight house and twenty-six stall roundhouse was completed by the Milwaukee Railroad in 1918 at a cost of $800,000.00. Steam engines were serviced twenty-four hours a day. When the roundhouse turntable was full of steam engines, revved at high speed, the windows in our farm house rattled; the engine noise so loud it was necessary to stand next to a family member when talking to them to hear the spoken words.

The slower freight trains were side-tracked right across from our farm when the Union Pacific stream-liners traveled over the tracks—City of Los Angeles, City of San Francisco, City of Denver, City of Portland, and Milwaukee Road's passenger trains *Hiawatha* and *Arrow*. All of them passed our farm at speeds of ninety miles an hour. Father checked his pocket watch to see if the trains were on time, and checked with the Atkins railroad agent, he knew personally, about any situations that caused their delay. The trains were always on time leaving Chicago's Union Station, and only a short time was required to reach our eastern Iowa location.

"It's just the railroad making noise. Go back to sleep!" Father got out of bed and went to each bedroom when we were awakened in the night by the loud railroad noise. Steam engines were the mainstay of the railroads in the 1930's and were on the turntable twenty-four hours a day, revved with a noise that at night wakened our family. It was many years later that the Milwaukee Railroad shut down 1,500 miles of trackage in Iowa.

I was a teenager before I learned the constant noise in my ears is "tinnitus." Until then I thought everyone heard noise in their ears. Tinnitus remains with me all the days of my life, a result of my birth and all my young life so close to the large railroad center where excess noise was a constant twenty-four hours a day.

The house I was born in was built in 1908–09. The foundation made of stone native to the area. The house did not have plumbing, and the kitchen had wainscoting around the walls. The basement had a wood burning furnace for central heating. There were five bedrooms: four upstairs, and the one bedroom downstairs where I was born. The kitchen had a washroom on the south side. There was one closet in the house, a walk-in closet on the second floor used for storage of out-of-season clothing. In autumn, storm windows and storm doors were put on the house to protect it from winter weather though ice still froze on the inside of window panes during below zero temperatures. Approximate outdoor temperatures could be told by looking at the amount of ice on the windows.

Grandpa sold the farm we lived on to my father in 1942. After father finished paying for the farm, he remodeled the kitchen and enclosed the screened-in porch. Wainscoting was removed from the kitchen walls, new doorways cut from the kitchen into the washroom, and from the dining room into the living room. Walls were re-plastered, cabinets and countertops installed in the kitchen with plumbing and a double sink. A new electric range replaced the iron cook stove. The remodeled kitchen was all-white with white appliances, and inlaid linoleum covered the floor; typical of modern kitchens of that era. A bathroom with bathtub was installed upstairs by dividing in half one of the four second-floor bedrooms. I was in high school when all this was completed.

Iowa farm house where Margaret Krug was born.

CHAPTER 2
Siblings

    I recall my younger sister trying to pronounce the word, "Popocatépetl." It resulted in both of my sisters, one four years older than me and one four years younger than me, all trying to pronounce that word. Mother started the word pronunciation when there was little for us to do except argue with each other. She taught eight elementary grades in a public school before her marriage, and she often used teachable moments with her growing children when it was of interest or helpful to the situation. Mexico's mountain, 5,526 foot Popocatépetl, was one of the fun times when laughter broke out as we struggled to say the word the way mother said it should be pronounced. It was a constructive activity that was thought provoking, and it kept us occupied.

    My older sister and I were sent outdoors every day to play in the middle of both the morning and afternoon. It was another practice mother continued from her school teaching days that was like a recess for her, and allowed her some uninterrupted time for household and farm work.

    When I was too young to initiate the outdoor play, my older sister positioned me in the backyard to stand still and wait while she herded a gaggle of geese eating around the house-yard. She walked behind the geese and chased them up to me causing them to spread out their flapping wings and make noise, and they knocked me to the ground. I cried so loud mother heard me in the house, or where she was working, and ran to pick me up. It happened so often that mother finally talked father into discontinuing the raising of geese. The goose house was in the orchard and had been the large cupola on the barn when Grandpa bought the farm. He removed the cupola and replaced it with a smaller medal cupola that still exists on the barn as this is written. When all the geese were gone, mother converted the large cupola that housed them into a "play house" for children, and she furnished it with a small table and chairs.

Play time in my youth was creative and required little equipment. When cousins visited our farm we played "Kick the Can" and "Hopscotch." When we tired of those games we chose sides and tossed a ball over the big corn-crib while yelling, "Red Rover, Red Rover send (name of a player) right over." We waited to see if the ball had been caught before the two sides completely exchanged location, causing the named person to be out of the game. We played until the last two persons tossed the ball over the building. It was a fun challenge in our young lives.

Sometimes many cousins were present for family reunions or winter card playing by the adults and the children were sent upstairs to a bedroom so their noise was not easily heard. We played "Button, button, who's got the button?" All that was needed to play was a ball of string large enough to go around the hands of everyone standing in a circle, and a button. Everyone moved their hands back and forth across the string carefully to be undetected while pushing a button strung on it from one person to the next person. The one designated "it" had to watch and determine where the button was hiding. If the person with the button was caught, that person became "it." We enjoyed that game.

When children were together in winter, and there was new fallen snow, we played "Fox and Geese" by walking in single file to make a trail circle twenty feet or more in diameter. In single file we walked across the circle from one border to the other, then at right angles to the first diameter; that made four pieces of "pie," half way between the two diameters. We stomped out two "rest" areas and selected one person to be "it" that chased the others, positioned around the diameter. If "it" caught a player, that player became "it." To escape being caught a player could duck into a "rest" area. A player became "it" if he or she stepped into the pie, or stepped out of bounds. It was a fast game with lots of yelling that we often played in the snowy winter months.

    My older sister's favorite place to play was the barn haymow. I was never excited about playing there because I climbed up into the haymow every day to gather eggs where at least one hen had a nest where she always hid her eggs. It was my responsibility to gather all the eggs daily; that required going everywhere in buildings around the farmstead. My older sister, much taller and larger, insisted on playing in the haymow, her favorite way to pass idle time. We jumped in the hay after enough of it was used so there was space between the roof of the mow, and the location of the ladder to the platform used for adjusting the rope that pulled the hay across the length of the barn.

    I was not as brave as my older sister in climbing the hand-over-hand ladder on the back barn wall to stand on the small pulley platform just under the roof. She enjoyed jumping off the little platform into the hay, but I always balked when it was my turn to climb the ladder so my sister pushed me to the bottom rung, then shoved her leg into my back to force me up onto the next ladder rung. She climbed behind me all the way so I could not turn back. Up on the platform I refused to jump, and she reached over from the ladder and shoved me off into the hay.

    One day my older sister led me to the hog house, one of the lowest buildings on the farm, and she figured out how to climb from the fence attached to it to get up onto the roof.

She coaxed me to join her on the roof which required her help. When we were both on the roof she decided to "fly" by jumping off, but she wanted me to try it first. She demonstrated how to flap my arms like a bird. After showing me how to "fly" she shoved me off the roof, and I fell straight to the ground with such an impact that my loud screams and crying were heard by mother where she was at work in the garden.

Mother ran to help me to the house and scolded my older sister for climbing on the hog house roof. Years later it was discovered my collarbone had been broken at a young age, and it may have happened in falls in the barn or from the hog house. My parents never discovered that it was broken because every time I cried my older sister would say, "There's nothing wrong with Margaret, she's crying just to be crying."

My Iowa State University professor of family life studies assigned students to write a paper on the subject of siblings that included a follow-up professor conference to aid in the teaching and understanding about family life. I wrote about the happenings with my older sister. When she reviewed my paper with me in conference she explained I had experienced "sibling rivalry," a term previously unknown to me. It was a new term to me and it helped my understanding of the happenings with my older sister in my youth.

Mother wrote in the "baby book" that she kept about me that when I was one year of age, and it was my older sister's fifth birthday, I was learning to walk and pulled myself up to stand by holding onto the doorknobs of the lower kitchen cupboards. My older sister noticed that my standing attracted mother's attention so she ran and pushed me down so hard my face hit the wooden floor and knocked out my whole front tooth including the root. I still have that tooth with its long root that is fastened in my "Baby Book" that mother gave me in her later years.

Mother explained to me that my older sister was jealous of all the attention she gave me after my birth when she nursed me. When school started that September she sent my sister to public school first grade at the age of four years because she already knew how to read. Mother had spent so much time reading with her, before I was born, that my older sister learned to read by four years of age.

There were always intriguing ideas for siblings to try in my youth. One I recall was squeezing lemon juice and using it to write a secret letter. My older sister had read about Benedict Arnold writing secret letters with lemon juice. We squeezed lemon juice, but had difficulty trying to decipher "lemon juice words" after they were written. It was not very successful.

My older sister had a dog in the years before I was born, and it no longer existed. In my youth my father's friend gave him a dog named "Teddy" that slept in a box behind the kitchen stove and went to the kitchen door when he wanted to go outdoors. Every time Teddy came to wherever I was sitting in the kitchen and looked up at me, that was all he needed to do, and I knew it meant he wanted to go outside. I never touched Teddy, but immediately got up and opened the kitchen door and let him out of the house and out of the porch screen door.

"He's not your dog!" my older sister yelled angrily at me every time she saw the dog going to me. Her yelling got mother's attention, and mother explained the dog belonged to our father and not to any of the children. That calmed my sister temporarily, but never stopped her from repeating her accusations every time Teddy went to me. He never went to my older sister when he wanted out of the kitchen.

My father knew animals go to some people and not to others, and as I grew to teenage years he asked me to assist with the farm animals. He requested I lead the horses from their barn stalls to drink in the water tank in the lower yard, and then return them to their barn stall. I opened the gates to put the cows in the barn, put the milking machine on them, and the cows never kicked.

When I went away from home to study in college I wrote a letter every week to my parents, and also continued that in later years. My parents shared my letters with my sisters, and they continued to know about my life. In our adult years, we three sisters went together to the Holy Land, to Europe and Tangiers, Africa via Gibraltar.

CHAPTER 3
Education

Memories of my early school years are surreal. *"What is black and white and red all over?"* my older sister teased me to find out if I knew the answer: *"newspaper."* Then she would ask me to spell Mississippi to see if I could do it. She insisted I needed to know those two things when I started to school, but my first day at school at age five years I was not required to answer either of what she said I needed to know. There was a difference between where she went to Fremont Township's Public School, soon after I was born, and where I went to our church parochial school my first eight grades.

My father made the decision about the school I attended since mother made the decision to send my older sister to a public school like she had taught in before her marriage. Kindergarten was not a state requirement in elementary schools at the time I started to school so my first year I was in first grade. I went to the same school my father attended in his youth, and I had the same head teacher he had in his school years.

Father was taught in the German language, and he began to learn English as a subject in grade school. I learned to write in script by the "Palmer Method," the same as my father had learned it in his school years. The head teacher was very critical of cursive writing and often called the student attempts at writing vertical up and down as 'chicken scratching'.

Religion was part of my school days as the apostle Paul wrote to Timothy (2 Timothy 1:3) "I thank God whom I serve....I have remembrance of thee in my prayers night and day." Every school day began with the ringing of the school bell at 9 a.m. followed by the singing of a hymn, and the children standing to recite "The Apostles Creed." Daily, after lunch, we read a chapter out of the Bible by taking turns with a different student reading each verse. "Memory work" was assigned for each school day from either the hymnal or Martin Luther's Small Catechism. When a student did not know their memory work they were given a "sawbuck" in teacher's grade book.

In good weather, my first four grades, I walked the two and a half miles to the parochial school, located next to the rural church that was similar to the Christian Day School in my family's native village of Löhlbach, Germany. I wished for a "hack," the name of transportation other students had when they were transported by car each day. When weather conditions were not favorable, father arranged for our neighbor, also his cousin, to transport me by car along with their older daughter though I had to walk from our farm the quarter of a mile each way to their farm for the ride.

In first grade I had only two classmates; one was my six year old cousin whose parents held her back a year to start to school with me, otherwise she would have been the only student in her grade. The other classmate was a large five year old boy. I was smaller than my two classmates and my teacher, the daughter of the head teacher, held me on her lap in reading class. One classmate stood on her left and one on her right side. We took turns reading out loud out of the same book and the teacher turned the book to each student when it was their turn to read. When it was my turn, the book was turned so the right side was up for me to read, but I already knew the sentence I was to read because I had read it upside down while following what my classmates were slowly reading. Learning to read upside down at that young age made it possible for me to read words and sentences upside down all my life.

Music class was an hour each morning and I memorized words of songs assigned every week. In first grade I sang a solo in the Christmas Eve program at church, and many of the older people that attended sat in pews close to the front, and came up immediately after the end of the program to thank me for my singing. I did not realize until years later that many of the elderly people in the congregation were also my German relatives.

Sanitary facilities at the rural school, when it was located in the country, were two gray wooden structures located between the congregation's cemetery and the ball diamond. Water for the school classrooms was provided by a pump on the schoolhouse grounds, and a large earthenware crock with a spigot in each classroom. Each student kept a folding cup in their desk for their drinking.

The 4th of July it was traditional to have an all-church picnic on the church and school grounds. The men of the congregation played a ball game after the meal and a program was held on an outside stage on the south side of the church. I sang the solo "God Bless America" at the last 4th of July congregation picnic of the rural church, built in 1891, that was torn down when I was in the fourth grade at the school located next to it. The church stained glass windows were not saved, and students picked up the glass pieces from the windows that fell to the ground. I have two round glass pieces from those windows, one gold color and one that is clear glass that I saved from the church where I was baptized. The shaped supports of the white balcony railing upstairs in the church were discarded and I have two of them, each with a stand on the bottom that made them into large candle holders and they have been standing on each side of the fireplace in our downstairs family room.

The summer before my fifth grade, the rural parochial school structure was moved into the small town of Atkins, and I either walked or rode a bicycle the one mile to school from our farm home. In bitter, cold winter weather father drove me to school, and the sight of him driving up to the school at the time classes let out in the afternoon was a warning that the weather was severe, or going to be soon, and he did not want me to walk home.

"Margaret. Is the school choir singing this Sunday?" father inquired.

The parochial school choir sat in the choir loft in front of the church where it was possible to view the entire congregation. Father sang in the parochial school choir when he was a student and he made sure I attended every Sunday the choir was performing. He went to church every Sunday, sometimes to the German language service held earlier in the morning, when mother could not attend due to frequent nasal and throat "sinus trouble." In my mind's eye, I can still see father sitting next to Great-Uncle John or his father's bachelor Uncle Bill, or his Uncle George who was only eleven years older than he was. They sat together every Sunday.

The church bell sometimes tolled during school hours, and school students counted the number of times it tolled to guess who in the congregation had died. One toll rang out for each decade of the person's age, followed by a pause, followed by tolling of each additional year of age of the person. When a funeral was held in the church, the bell tolled continuously from the moment the casket exited the church door, at the conclusion of the service, until the funeral procession arrived at the church cemetery, a tradition that began with the burial of my immigrant ancestors to accompany their departed soul to eternal rest. The church bell was tolled at six o'clock every Saturday evening as a reminder of the approach of the Sabbath Day.

Somewhere between the first snowflake of the season and Christmas there were many practices during school hours for the church Christmas Eve program. Memorizing a "piece" to recite in the program, all my eight elementary school years, was practiced with my mother. I learned and loved to sing the song, "Jerusalem" in the first grade. The words, "One night as I lay sleeping I dreamed a dream so fair. I stood in Old Jerusalem beside the temple"...a word picture for me. In those early years of my life it became my desire to one day travel to Jerusalem.

My elementary teacher taught us to believe in Jesus as the son of God the Father, and I prayed to be saved to eternal life. I was taught that when the Holy Spirit entered my life I would know by the grace of God about my salvation. I prayed and prayed remembering the Bible verse Matthew 20:16 – "for many are called, but few chosen." It happened one winter morning when I walked on our farm driveway toward the mailbox to pick up the mail. A puddle of water in the driveway car tracks was frozen into ice. I was not wearing overshoes and slid back and forth across the ice on my leather shoe soles. Suddenly when I was in the air, not pushing myself across the ice, something I had done many times, I was filled with a joy that I had never known before or known since that time. I suddenly felt the Holy Spirit was with me and I no longer had fear about my salvation. It was a miracle. Awareness of the presence of The Holy Spirit has been with me since that day in my life.

Every Christmas Eve father cleaned the barn so all the animals had clean bedding and an extra ration of food. He told me the farmers in his family practiced this from the time they emigrated from Germany. We observed three days of Christmas. Christmas Day was for individual family observance. Second Christmas Day was the reunion with grandparents and aunts, uncles and first cousins. Grandpa provided the stuffed goose for the traditional potluck menu followed by a "name-drawn" gift exchange, and the grandchildren played the traditional German genealogy game with each cousin taking a turn at reciting the full name and birth date of each first cousin. Third Christmas Day we celebrated with favorite cousins; a potluck followed by hours of card games.

    I studied geography for the first time in the third grade. *Around The World with the Children* authored by Frank G. Carpenter remained my favorite book. Parochial school students had to purchase all the books they used, and I liked my first geography book so much that it has remained on my desk all my years, and it is still there as I write this manuscript. My teacher wrote my name in it in beautiful, perfect handwriting.

    September of my fourth grade the head teacher saw my bleeding nose every morning when I arrived after walking to school, and he laid me down on a bench and placed a cold wet cloth over my forehead to stop the nosebleed so I could participate in the nine a.m. opening of school. Another morning as I stood at my desk reciting my daily assigned memory work, with the head teacher at my side checking my recitation, he placed his hand on my right shoulder and discovered something of concern. He instructed me to tell my parents when I returned home that afternoon to take me to the doctor. Father finished farm chores early that evening and we drove to the next rural town to the doctor's office. We waited in line in a room full of people to take our turn to get in to see the doctor, and he diagnosed I had a broken collarbone. He placed my shoulders in a brace and gave me return appointments. The brace was so tight it wore sores under both of my arm pits, and I could not wear my new school dresses that year because they did not have enough space to accommodate the heavy brace.

My right shoulder did not change each time the doctor examined me over the next months, and he decided surgery was necessary. Mother objected to surgery right away when she learned I would need a long recovery from bone surgery, which could cause me to fall behind in school. I continued to wear the shoulder brace the remainder of that school year and it stopped the bleeding of my nose when I arrived at school each morning. Swinging my arms while I walked had caused the broken bones to press on my neck artery, which caused my nose to bleed.

At the end of the school year I had surgery to remove a cartilage movable joint formed by the two broken overlapping pieces of the collarbone. The surgeon performing the operation was not an orthopedist, and could not graft the broken collarbone pieces together. I was in the hospital a week with mother sleeping in my hospital room at night because of a severe ether reaction I had from surgery. I recovered in bed at home all summer with restriction to not move while the cut ends of the collarbone healed. Our doctor visited me in our home several times during the recovery.

I affirmed my baptismal faith through the rite of confirmation in the eighth grade and passed Benton County examinations for admittance to Atkins Fremont Township High School. Travel to high school was by bus every day, and we lived only a mile from the school so I was the first one to board the bus at 7:30 a.m. and rode the entire route every morning. The bus traveled the same route when school closed in the afternoon, and I liked being the first one to get off.

I practiced for the high school girls' basketball team and immediately became a first team substitute. My five foot, five inch height (taller than nearly all of the other high school girls) put me in demand as a guard substitute. My senior year I was the tallest girl on the girls' basketball first team.

High School general science class taught "ontogeny recapitulates phylogeny" I would never forget it, and my classmates repeated it over and over—the evolutionary development of an organism or species of plant or animal.

The Fremont Friendly Workers Girls 4-H Club was the only community activity for girls. I joined when I was twelve years old, the minimum age at that time. At age fifteen, when Benton County 4-H Girls Clubs studied home furnishings as the project of the year, I was elected Secretary of the Benton County 4-H Girls, and attended the 4-H State Convention on the Iowa State College campus, later named Iowa State University.

My parents gave me my own room for the first time and I could decorate and furnish it for my 4-H home furnishings project. The room had never been finished when the house was built in 1908. It was the fourth bedroom on the second floor, which had previously been used as a storage room with rough, unfinished floor boards dotted with black spots of oozing sap from the use of green lumber at the time the house was built. The plastered walls had never been sized for final finish. Inserted pins protruded from the wall that lacked molding strips to complete the trim needed to hang wall pictures.

Blue was my favorite color and I painted the walls of my room blue. My closet was a board nailed across the picture molding behind the door of the room and a sheet draped around it to enclose a space large enough to hang clothes behind the door. The record I kept of restoring, decorating, and furnishing the room was selected the outstanding Benton County 4-H Home Furnishings project of the year, and I was awarded a gold commemorative medal at the Benton County 4-H Awards Banquet.

Mother taught me to sew at twelve years of age when I began fashioning clothing for my dolls. She did not have time to sew, but she agreed I could use her treadle sewing machine. I managed to immediately run the sewing machine needle through the last joint of my middle finger on my left hand as I tried to guide the tiny pieces of cloth to stitch close to the edge. The needle broke off in my finger bone with the needle sticking out of both sides of my finger. Mother used a pair of pliers to pull the two pieces out, and I continued sewing on the treadle machine. In a short time I was sewing clothing for myself.

When clothing was the 4-H project for the year I sewed for my school wardrobe and also for both of my sisters' wardrobes, and made dresses for my mother. That clothing project was chosen as the most outstanding Benton County 4-H Girls Clothing Project, and I was awarded a gold medal from a major textile company at the Benton County 4-H Awards Banquet that year.

I teamed with a 4-H club member to give a demonstration at the Benton County Fair and practiced nearly every day that summer with my teammate and our 4-H leader, a retired English teacher who also taught us public speaking. In our community of predominately German families, dishes were not rinsed in hot water before wiping them dry. Our demonstration showed sanitary methods of dish washing and we named it "Dish Washing Can Be Fun." We presented our demonstration to every woman's group in the township that summer. We used vinegar in the rinse water to make glassware sparkle, and soaked pots and pans in cleaning soda.

There were demonstration teams from every township in Benton County at the Benton County Fair, and my teammate and I were judged the champion 4-H Benton County demonstration team. We were recognized with our photo published in Benton and Linn County newspapers. The Iowa State Fair had been suspended for the duration of World War II; therefore, we were unable to compete any further.

My 4-H leader was director of the annual Benton County 4-H Girls Camp and she chose me as her assistant, which required going with her to a regional camp training school each spring that was organized by the Iowa Extension Service Recreation Program. Each July we held a week of 4-H Girls Camp at the Palisades State Park until the State 4-H Camp was completed in the center of the state. It was a great leadership experience for me. I am thankful to 4-H and the youth development programs of the Iowa State Extension Service for making a difference in my life at a young age.

My 4-H leader, a retired English teacher, trained me in public speaking and, in my senior year, I won the Atkins High School speech contest and gave my speech on a Cedar Rapids, Iowa, WMT radio broadcast. In my high school senior year I was chosen to play the leading role in our high school class play.

Music was an enjoyable part of all of my school years, and I always looked forward to participating in musical programs. I wanted to play in the band and my mother decreed I must play a trombone using the same one my older sister played in her high school years. Mother said I had no choice of another instrument as the trombone was what our family owned, and if I wanted to be in the band that was what I had to play.

A Different World

    My high school freshman year the band teacher was the same one my older sister had in high school. My first trombone lesson, the teacher discovered I had crooked front teeth and said I could not play a trombone because my upper lip would split as it pulled tight over the crooked teeth to form the notes. I told mother what the band teacher said, but she refused to accept that reason and ordered me to continue the trombone if I wanted to be in the band. I wanted to continue but the band teacher forbid me to become a member of the band or to go to the band contests held that year. I wrote my own trombone lessons to practice notes on the music scale until I could play them. A trombone has a slide, not valves, and when the slide is moved with the arm it is necessary to tongue notes by saying syllables like "da" or "ta." It is necessary to say them fast going "da da da da" or "ta ta ta ta." I learned to tongue the notes by many hours of practice by myself.

    Atkins High School had a new band teacher the next year. The fact that my father was elected to the high school board made it possible for me to play in the high school band the remainder of those school years. I played first trombone; however, my freshman music teacher was right that my lip would split every time I tried to reach certain notes or play really loud.

    Fortunately, my cousin was a freshman at Atkins High School my sophomore year and he played a trombone. Since I could not play loud, as first trombones often do, I asked him take over at that point in the music. He liked doing it and that made it possible for me to continue playing first chair in the band. The night I graduated from high school the band played the opening program number. Then I laid my trombone down on my chair and walked up the stairs to sit on the stage for the graduation ceremony. I never again picked up the trombone to play another note. "To The

Valiant Heart Naught Is Impossible," was the theme of my graduation class.

When it was time to award graduates their high school diploma, the superintendent asked my father to come forward to the center of the stage and be introduced as the president of the Atkins School Board. The superintendent handed my diploma to my father and requested he present it to me. I was the first in my class to receive a diploma. It was a moment that made a difference in my life realizing my father had never graduated from high school because there was not a high school in the community in his youth. He studied arithmetic another year after eighth grade with a local teacher because of his interest in math. When he met my mother, a teacher, he was enrolled in Cedar Rapids Business College and graduated from their business course.

Atkins held summer band concerts outdoors on Main Street once a week. I played the trombone in them during my high school years with the help of my cousin sitting next to me playing his trombone really loud. John Philip Sousa's famous marches were brisk and exuberant and required loud trombone notes and were a joy that stayed with me all my years. "The Stars and Stripes Forever," "The Washington Post," and "Semper Fidelis," played every summer, have never been forgotten because I enjoyed them so much.

My interest in music included singing with the Atkins High School Girls Glee Club, and listening on the radio every week for two hours of music: "The Longines Symphonette," classical music sponsored by the Longines watch company with introductory theme, the final movement of Beethoven's 5th Symphony," and "The Bell Telephone Hour" featuring the best in classical and Broadway music with Jascha Heifetz, Marian Anderson, Bing Crosby, Nelson Eddy, Benny Goodman, Jose' Iturbi, Fritz Kreisler, Oscar

Levany, Ezio Pinza, Lily Pons, Gladys Swarthout, and Helen Traubel.

I enjoyed listening to Kate Smith singing, "When the Moon Comes over the Mountain," "God Bless America" and many songs she made famous. I have not forgotten the "Four-Leaf Clover" and "Dreaming;" songs learned and sang often in 4-H clubs.

The last Sunday in August, the summer I graduated from Atkins High School, my older sister married and I was Maid of Honor in her wedding. A large reception was held following the ceremony. There was nobody to help my father set up the tables and chairs in the church basement for the reception dinner, and I was his only help lifting all the tables and unfolding chairs, putting on table cloths, setting the tables and helping mother prepare food for the dinner reception. That day turned out to be the hottest, highest temperature day of summer, and I was exhausted by the time I dressed for the ceremony. My work was not finished until the reception cleanup was completed.

Through all the years of my youth, mother suggested I plan to go to college and it became my permanent plan. My college freshman year my parents decided that I should enroll at Bethany College, Mankato, Minnesota, where my older sister had studied one year. That college had a curriculum that did not meet my interests. Though I completed one year of freshman English and a semester each of botany and zoology; all other courses completed that year became electives toward my future degree.

The only moments that remain in my memory of my freshman year at Bethany College are the presidential election year campaign of autumn, when President Harry Truman came to Mankato for a whistle stop speech from his campaign train caboose platform. I walked downtown to see and hear for the first time a USA President.

The next academic year I enrolled at Iowa State College, now Iowa State University, to study for a bachelor's degree. I had been on the Iowa State campus as a teenager attending a 4-H girls' convention and knew from that time that it was where I wanted to study. When I was accepted at Iowa State my mother contacted a Benton County Extension Agent to find out if I could work for my board and room while a student at Iowa State. The only other required expense for Iowa residents was a $30.00 registration fee for each of three quarters in the scholastic year.

I received a letter from the Iowa Extension Home Economics Director on the Iowa State campus that enclosed the name of a seamstress in the city of Ames in need of a live-in student to prepare meals and do housework. I could live with her and earn my board and room while a student on campus. Recommendations by my Benton County Extension agents gave me the job.

My parents drove me to the residence of the seamstress for the first time the day September registration began on the campus. Father gave me $30.00 each month of the fall term to pay the cost necessary to ride a bus from the seamstress's home to the campus to class each day.

Fall term weeks passed and with the approach of the holidays the work of the seamstress increased. She used my bedroom for a fitting room for her many clients. I did not have a place, other than the bathroom, for studying that I needed to do. The seamstress suggested I spend evenings keeping her retired husband company in the living room while she had evening client fittings.

Chemistry was a difficult class for me because Atkins High School did not teach chemistry. Hours of laboratory work were required. My first applied art course also required long laboratory time leaving barely time for me to arrive at the seamstress's home to prepare the evening meals.

A Different World

I did not eat lunch and went to study at the campus library because I had little time for it in the seamstress's home.

Every week the seamstress added more tasks for me to do—household grocery shopping, ride her bicycle to deliver her finished garments to the address of clients in the city. The seamstress suggested I enroll in fewer courses so I would have more time for her work. It became evident that working for my board and room in her home would make completion of a degree difficult.

I went to the Registrar's Office to inquire what it cost to live in a dormitory on campus the next quarter, and discovered the rent for a dormitory room was $30.00 for each three month term. That was the cost of one month of bus tickets to ride each week to the campus from the seamstress's home. I realized I needed to move into a campus dormitory, and to find a job on campus to pay for my meals.

When it was time to travel home for November Thanksgiving weekend, my father sent me money to take the train to Cedar Rapids where he met me. I packed most of my clothing to take home to minimize what I had at the seamstress's home. When I returned to her home after the holiday, I notified the seamstress that I no longer would work for her after the end of the fall school term. I packed the remainder of my belongings to accompany me home for Christmas vacation.

I went to the Student Union on campus and applied for and was accepted to work in their cafeteria beginning winter term. There were openings for me to work for breakfast daily, and for some weekday evening meals. I went to the library on campus and applied for and was accepted to work at the circulation desk after my winter term class hours each day. I was limited in number of hours because of my class schedule hours, but I was paid in cash, which was helpful.

Winter and spring terms I got up at 4:30 a.m. every morning to leave my campus dormitory and set up the cafeteria line at the Student Union before it opened at 6:30 a.m. for breakfast. I served food in the cafeteria line, and ate a fast breakfast because I had an 8 a.m. class and I had to walk to it on the opposite side of the campus.

My library work at Iowa State's Parks Library was rewarding in that I met many students and professors. I enjoyed the palette of colors on the original Grant Wood murals in the library rotunda. I knew about Grant Wood because he lived in Cedar Rapids where I had visited his studio, and he studied at Coe College, the same campus where my mother was a student in her youth.

I chose textiles and clothing as my major field at Iowa State. My major counselor/professor removed me from clothing construction courses when she learned of my expertise in 4-H clothing projects, my winning clothing entries at the Iowa State Fair, and my county awards for Best Clothing Project in Benton County. My major field classes were devoted to design with its many facets and clothing aesthetics. I was accepted into my major field for a bachelor's degree when I easily passed the required freehand drawing class that used live models.

My historic textiles professor was outstanding. I learned so much from her that was "life-long learning." She had been a curator at the Egyptian Museum in Cairo at a time when it was possible to remove artifacts from that country. She had a variety of pieces of mummy cloths mounted on contrasting paper, and students were assigned to analyze the fiber content and weave of each piece. We were not allowed to touch the mummy cloths, and could only look at them closely through a magnifying glass, thus my study of textiles of many cultures of the world began with Egypt's oldest textiles.

As the years passed, and I visited museums in many countries, I recalled what I had learned in my major field about their culture and textiles. A Moroccan embroidery paper I wrote while studying for a degree included design diagrams and was helpful in understanding their culture when I was in that country.

The summer between my junior and senior years, a friend in my major field and my roommate knew a person who worked one summer in the Berkshire Hills of Massachusetts and who encouraged us to apply for work at the same resort. We applied and were accepted. Then we found a married couple on campus from Massachusetts, also students at Iowa State, driving home for the summer and they agreed the three of us could ride with them if we paid for their gas. It was my first time to see the states east of Chicago, and my first time to go to Niagara Falls where we stopped to ride 'The Maid of the Mist" up to the falls. In later years I would ride up to Niagara Falls two more times on "The Maid of the Mist."

Weekends at Eastover Estates in the Berkshire Hills there was time to travel and see western Massachusetts. Work finished the first of September and we rode a bus to Boston to tour historic sites, and traveled on a boat across to Provincetown, Cape Cod. The highlight of my time in Boston was going to Harvard University to see their famous collection of glass flowers in the Natural History Museum. They were made in Germany from 1887 through 1936 to aid in teaching botany when Harvard was the global center of botanical study. The 4,400 glass models look amazingly real, and no one has been able to duplicate the artistry in the flower collection. I felt privileged to see them.

We rode a bus to New York City and stayed in a Times Square hotel. We went to the top of the Empire State Building for a view of the city, and rode a ferry to the Statue of Liberty where I climbed the many steep steps to look out the windows in the crown of Lady Liberty and saw a fantastic view of the harbor. We went to Radio City to a performance of the Rockettes. We walked to St. Patrick's Cathedral to observe the architecture we had studied in cathedral architecture design in my major field. We rode another bus to see the Cathedral of St. John the Divine, the fourth largest Christian cathedral in the world.

I saved $50 to pay the cost of a one-way airplane ticket to fly from JFK Airport to Chicago, a new non-stop flight that year, and a first for the airlines. I had just enough money left from summer work to buy a train ticket from Chicago to Iowa, where my parents met me.

My major field professor/counselor planned my course schedule so I could graduate in three years at Iowa State. She gained permission from an Iowa State's dean for me to parallel courses, those required before others could be studied. My heavy class schedule made it necessary to quit working on campus my senior year to devote full time to classwork and studying. My father agreed to pay my senior year expenses when he learned I would graduate at the end of that year. It was my most rewarding year of university study when I found that paralleling courses made them more meaningful though I had to devote many more hours of study to complete all the required assignments.

My senior year at Iowa State my major field professor/counselor called me in for a conference to tell me the textiles and clothing faculty had chosen me for graduate study following the receiving of my bachelor's degree. I would be the first student permitted to go direct to graduate school without having worked in the field several years before returning to study for a graduate degree. She said it would be a two year program, and I needed $3,000 to finance my first year of graduate study that extended through the summer term. Iowa State would pay for my second year of study for the graduate degree.

"Does your father own his farm?" my major field professor/counselor inquired.

"Yes," I replied.

"An Iowa farmer who owns his farm can send his daughter to Iowa State for $3,000 to obtain a master's degree. Go home and inquire and let me know the decision." she said.

I went home and told my mother about the opportunity Iowa State was giving me to continue studying two years for a master's degree, and that I needed $3,000 for the first year of study, and Iowa State would pay for the second year.

"Don't you talk to your father about it or I'll see to it you are disinherited," mother answered.

She said if my father had $3,000 he was not investing in farming, she wanted it to travel to Israel to the Holy Land. Her response was a shock to me and I no longer pursued the idea.

Margaret Krug Palen

CHAPTER 4
Farm Years

My father reminded me many times, "You were my first crop on the farm!" My grandparents bought the farm in 1930, and my parents took possession of it March 1, 1931. I was born when my twenty-six year old father was planting the last field of his first corn crop on the farm. He had to stop his last planting and go to the house and call the doctor that arrived within fifteen minutes for my birth.

The growing season for corn to mature between frosts in Iowa is ninety days: between May 15 and September 15. Iowa corn uses less water than other grain crops, and creates little fertilizer runoff. The state of Iowa, for many years, was five hours of flat, corn-lined interstate highway between the Mississippi River and Nebraska state line, interrupted only by an occasional rural town or city.

The "Great Depression" was soaring in my childhood years. My paternal grandparents' economic success was due to their family's constant hard work. Grandpa was the eldest of ten children and Grandma was the eldest daughter of ten children. My father had one hundred first cousins. My paternal grandparents invested early in farm land and banking, and their grandchildren were born during the "Great Depression" when many other families could not afford to have children.

"How could you afford to have me born?" I inquired of my father when there were three in my grade school class, and twelve in my high school class and four of them were my cousins.

"We had money to pay the doctor to deliver you, and enough to raise you," father replied.

The farm where I was born was known as "a Krug Brothers farm." My father's initials and name were painted on the red barn in large white letters below 1910, the year the barn was built. My father was one of four sons and my grandparents owned all the farms their sons lived on.

One of my never-forgotten memories of farm life is the song of the Western Meadowlark on the prairie in the spring and summer months. I associate it with the open spaces of my young life though their song is "a cadence of wild sadness"— whippor-will, whippor-will.

The year father retired from his farm, to the home he built just a mile west in Atkins, he gave me a memento of the farm I was born on: a double-tree equalizing bar used with a two horse team given to him by his father the year he moved to the farm. I have kept it propped up in a corner in my family room where I see it and am reminded of the farm.

In 1942, Grandpa realized his two youngest sons were of an age required to register for military service, and would be drafted in World War II. He decided to sell his farms to his sons so they would be landowners needed for the war effort, therefore, ineligible for military duty. My father's age made it necessary for him to register immediately with the first call of the local Draft Board.

I walked to the road gate mailbox to pick up the mail the day father's 1-A draft notice arrived. Mother opened the envelope since father was working in a field, and she began to cry realizing my father was called immediately to military service.

At lunch time, father came to the house and read his mail; however, he was not upset. He then revealed to us that

Grandpa had already arranged to sell the farm we lived on to him. That upset mother because she immediately thought of the cost of the farm, and the large amount of saving that would be necessary to pay for the land.

I was awakened early several mornings in my upstairs bedroom, located at the top of the second floor stairway, by the loud talking of my parents eating breakfast at 6 a.m., after the cows were milked, the cream separated, and the hogs and horses were fed. My parents argued about buying the farm. Mother's Scottish thrift prevailed, and father said everything he could think of to calm her emotions, but his voice sounded angrier every time he had to speak up about it. I never forgot the conflict going on in mother's mind about buying the farm we lived on. It was many years later, I learned that Grandpa set the sale price of the farm at half the amount he originally paid to purchase it in cash in the 1930's Great Depression.

World War II prices boomed, and father bought rubber tires and lights for his tractor to work in the fields at night, and he produced more crops to sell at high wartime prices. Father bought all his farm machinery from his Uncle August, owner of a Cedar Rapids farm equipment company, also his baptismal godfather, who gave him one of his middle names. Father always received good "trade-in" value for his machinery from his uncle. I learned within two years father paid off the debt he owed Grandpa for the farm.

Children ate breakfast alone whenever we got up on non-school days; on school days it was at 7:15 a.m. Mother made oatmeal early every morning for the parent's breakfast with sufficient quantity so there was plenty left over for children to eat. Slices of buttered toast, leftover from my parents' morning meal, were sitting on a plate waiting to be eaten. Mother made fried eggs with hard yolks for me for my breakfast. It was my job, from a young age, to daily gather all the eggs on the farm and I frequently ran into broken or cracked eggs that spilled on my hands. I couldn't stand the smell of the runny, yellow yolks, and my whole lifetime I have only eaten eggs with hard cooked yolks.

Foot tracks from the garden and barnyard work were frequent on the kitchen floor. Early memories of the farm house where I was born and raised include seeing newspapers on the kitchen floor. The kitchen had five doorways and mother scrubbed the floor and laid down old newspapers to walk on until the floor dried because someone in the family always needed to walk across the kitchen to get to the washroom, to the porch, to the downstairs bedroom, or to go upstairs to the bathroom, or downstairs into the basement. The linoleum in the kitchen had wood floor borders and needed a lot of water to scrub it clean, and it was slow to dry.

As I grew in the teenage years I helped mother with cooking and canning. It was an everyday task in summer to conserve the crops that mother raised in her large garden. She preserved food for the winter months by drying sweet corn and beans, and canned large amounts of home-grown peaches; 300-500 quarts of fruit: pears, elderberries, strawberries, raspberries, gooseberries, applesauce, cherries, plums, grapes; 300-400 quarts of vegetables: yellow wax beans, green string beans, sweet corn, carrots, peas, tomatoes, sauerkraut, kohlrabi, spinach, kale, horseradish, grape leaves, lime pickle sticks, piccalilli, and, bread and butter pickles. I picked all the fruit, shelled the peas, and cut the corn off the cob and anything else she wanted as she prepared the next step in the process.

A family activity I remember vividly was homemade sausage night. Each year, when cold weather set in, father and his brothers butchered several hogs and a steer. One night was set aside for a family gathering at our home when the men ground the pork and beef using the bench I sat on at mealtime to mount the grinder and sausage press. They blended the beef and pork together using Grandpa's recipe: garlic, salt, pepper, cloves, allspice, nutmeg. The men mixed and seasoned the meat using Grandpa's hands cupped together for measurement. Mother cooked a sample of the mixture to make sure it had the preferred flavor. When it tasted just right, it was pressed into sausage. A large cast iron sausage press, a black cylindrical devise, was filled with the blended meat and spices, and a large flat plate slowly cranked down onto the meat forcing it into natural sausage casings that were cleaned intestines. Each sausage was about two feet long. The casings were cut, the ends twisted and tied with a cord. A sausage fry with delicious aroma around midnight was fun for all the family, and one of the times children were privileged to stay up late to participate. The next day the sausage rings were hung to cure in a smokehouse on our farm.

When children were in school, my parents made headcheese, kopf kaise in the German language, from the hog head. The jowls, hog cheeks, were not used because they were too fat. The head was cooked until the meat could be taken off the bone. The tongue, heart, and liver were cooked and pressed through the meat grinder. Salt, pepper and small amounts of nutmeg, allspice, and cloves were added and mixed thoroughly, and cooked again for about one and one-half to two hours. Then it was poured into a shallow crock to cool, and later to be sliced. I never liked the taste of headcheese and never ate it. My parents ate all the headcheese for lunch on the days when children were in school.

My assigned farm job on spring, summer, and autumn days was to walk to a field (sometimes it was a half mile each way to the back forty acres, where the cows were grazing in a pasture) and to herd them back to the barnyard to the water tank, where they then were ready for evening milking.

    Summer mornings, when school was over, and father finished milking the cows, he moved them into the large farm building grass yard and closed the gate to the road. He wakened my older sister and me and asked us to herd the cows along the road ditches between our farm and west to the neighbors, a distance of a quarter mile. One of us sat by the road gate and made sure the cows did not venture east, and the other one walked west to the last hill before the neighbor's buildings and turned the cows around at that point to return east to our road-gate. The cows grazed on grass in the ditches on both sides of the road which kept the weeds down while helping to extend the pastures for the summer months.

    I often heard my father talking in the German language when he was working with the cattle in the farmyard around the barn area. He yelled at them in the German language. Father was bilingual and talked in both languages at the meal table when his brothers or when Grandpa ate in our home. Each of them could easily interchange words in the English and German language in the same sentence, however, Grandpa did not want his grandchildren to learn the German language and he required his sons to strictly enforce his decision. If a grandchild asked what the men were saying in the German language, the child was immediately sent out of the room with the reminder that they were only to know and speak the English language. The in-laws of all five of Grandpa's children only knew the English language which reinforced the use of, and made possible only the English language in the extended family.

A Different World

"Would you like to hear the corn grow?" father asked me one beautiful July day. He closely watched his corn crop.

"Yes." I replied, and was amazed at the question. Father walked me to the nearest field and into several rows of corn.

"Be quiet, and listen," father said. "That's green gold you're looking at! Green gold!" was father's description of his corn fields. The bounty of the beauty of the growing corn was a wealth in itself.

There was not a breeze or any air movement, and I could hear a snapping sound that was the corn growing taller. Father was right that it was possible to hear the corn grow, and I was amazed to learn that, and that I could hear it growing. Soon it would be taller than father's six foot height.

There were lightning rods on the house, barn, and corn-crib. Electrical summer storms raged when the yearly annual rainfall fell in the three months of the growing season—May 15 to September 15. There often were lightning strikes on our farm. We thought probably lightning was attracted to our farm because it was so close to the nearby large railroad center. Lightning strikes at night were very loud and caused father to get out of bed and walk to each bedroom to tell everyone in the family to go back to sleep. In later years, when father raised beef cattle for the Chicago market, he waited until morning to walk to the back forty acres where his Hereford feeder cattle were grazing to see if any of them had been struck by lightning.

"There's a letter from Grandpa B.!" I yelled to mother while running to the house from the mailbox located on our farm road driveway. I recognized the postmark from Salt Lake City, Utah. Mother was excited to find a letter from her father and immediately opened it. Several carefully folded newspaper clippings fell out. Grandpa always included newspaper items he thought would be of interest to our family. It is how I learned my maternal grandparents were educated teachers and an example for education in my life since my German relatives did not go to school beyond the eighth grade because there was not a high school in their Iowa community in those years of the century.

My maternal grandpa had been a school teacher, bank founder and cashier, farmer, newspaper editor and publisher, postal clerk and postmaster, store owner, hotel clerk, missionary and church elder.

When I was eight years old he arrived by streamliner train and brought his second wife to meet our family.

"I made a mistake when I divorced your grandfather," my maternal grandma often told me. "He is a good man. Don't ever do what your sister tells you to do. My sister told me to get a divorce because she wanted me to stay in Cedar Rapids and take care of your great-grandma who could no longer live alone."

The extra bedroom on the second floor of our farm home was where my maternal grandparents from Utah lived on visits to Iowa. Their train tickets were good for a year and they lived with us many months. Grandpa relived his farming years of owning three different farms when he put on a pair of my father's denim bib overalls and went along on the tractor with father to the fields on our farm.

Father promised my Utah maternal grandparents he would return their visit. The following summer, we drove through the Badlands of South Dakota and stopped in the Black Hills on our way to Salt Lake City. (Chapter 6)

When I was thirteen years old father took me to the oats field when the grain was ready for harvest, and he showed me how to drive his tractor on the binder without jerking it or turning so sharply the tractor could upset. I rode with him to open the oats field and he taught me how to make exact right-hand turns on each corner of the field enabling the binder to cut all the grain and not leave any of it standing in the corners. I drove the tractor on the binder to cut the oats with father sitting on the binder and dropping the bundles while two of his brothers, my uncles, made oat shocks across the field. It was years later when father and his younger brother went together and purchased a power combine.

Margaret with oat sheaves

Margaret Krug (center) at threshing time, delivering drinking water to the men.

Father went to Kansas City to buy young cattle to feed and sell on the Chicago market. While he was gone mother and I did all the chores on our farm. Father bought young Hereford steers and had them shipped by railroad to our farm. When they arrived, one was dead from "shipping fever" and another one was sick. A veterinary was called and the sick animal's health restored. The steers were fed for nine months, and father rode in the truck with the driver to ship them to the Chicago stockyards. The buyer of his cattle sent father in a limousine to return to his Iowa farm.

Summer vacation between my college years I painted the smaller buildings on my parents' farm to change their color from red to white when father decided he wanted all white farm buildings. A contractor painted the large barn and large elevator corn crib. I painted two coats of white paint on each building to change the red color they had been many years: cattle shed, hog house, chicken house, machine shed, and garage.

A Different World

W. W. Krug 1910 red barn.

Farm buildings, all painted white.

Indelible in my memory is the week I took over all the farm chores by myself so my parents could both go fishing in Minnesota with two other farm couples. My parents did not have anyone to do their chores and they wanted to go to their favorite Hibbing, Minnesota lake.

I was alone on the farm all that week and arose early each morning to stanchion the cows, milk them with a milking machine, and carry the milk to the house-yard shed to separate the cream. I carried the cream into the house basement to keep it cool in cold water until it was picked up by a creamery, and the skim milk I carried to feed the hogs. I watered the horses at the water tank in the lower barnyard. The cows I gated in a nearby field. It was August and the peach crop on the trees on the farm was ripe, and I picked peaches every day and canned them, which mother always did at that time.

All that work, by the end of the week, exhausted me. I did not appreciate the long hours of work on the farm though I learned about decision-making, problem-solving, and work-ethic responsibility. I made up my mind at that time that I never wanted to marry a farmer, and never wanted to live on a farm the remainder of my life. I never wavered from that decision.

My residence and work on the farm where I was born ended at age twenty-one years after I graduated from college.

CHAPTER 5
Employment

"When are you going to get a job?" father inquired of me the summer after I graduated with a bachelor's degree in textiles and clothing. He did not want me to become a salesclerk in a department store though my textiles degree qualified me for retailing, and new employees in that field often took jobs as a sales clerk.

Before graduation I applied on campus at Iowa State's Extension Service office to be a county extension agent. I knew about that work from my years in 4-H, and learned the interview board only met once a year. In the meantime, a classmate friend in my major field decided with me to find a job in Chicago, and save money to travel to Europe. We wanted to experience some of what we learned in our major field. My friend's father was president of a Cicero, Illinois, bank and worked with an employment agency that she knew would find us a job.

My father agreed with my going to Chicago, and gave me money to buy a train ticket, and a small amount of cash until I found a job. I arrived at my friend's home in a Chicago suburb, and immediately we both received interviews via her father's employment agency. We were each hired by a different Chicago business. Her father took me to a home in Oak Park to rent a sleeping room, with breakfast included, and I rode the train with a transfer to a bus to Western Felt Company on Ogden Avenue where I was hired as a chemist in charge of two technicians in the company's test laboratory.

My parents transferred a letter from the Iowa State campus sent to my home address that announced dates of the Extension Service Interview Board during Homecoming weekend. That Friday, after work, I boarded a streamliner in downtown Chicago's Union Station to ride to the Iowa campus. I stayed with students I knew previously, and interviewed for an Iowa Extension Service job.

The Iowa Extension Service Interview Board contacted my Western Felt Company employer, and immediately hired me in the interview as they could do at that time. They said I had taken a job instead of sitting around waiting for their interview. I returned to Western Felt Company to work until February to fulfill my obligation to work a minimum number of months or pay a forfeiture fee to the employment agency that arranged for my hiring for the Chicago job.

It was necessary to own a car for county extension service work in Iowa, and with my father's help I purchased a new Ford sedan. My beginning salary was low, and it was difficult scrimping and saving to repay my father each month until I paid him everything that I owed him for the car.

My employment as an Iowa county extension home economist with a Federal appointment began as a trainee in Linn County, and later I was assigned to Bremer County in the northern part of the state of Iowa. Each month I traveled to the Iowa State campus for 4-H training, adult education meetings, or to attend organization conventions.

I was on the campus a week each December for the Iowa Annual Extension Service Conference with its major objective as an "off-campus" educational activity to help people understand and apply scientific developments in agriculture and related sciences for a better life. My job was a life-interpreting discipline with a goal of the development of human potential, included organizing 4-H clubs that taught citizenship, leadership and critical thinking. I organized adult women's groups for continuing adult education to make a difference in their lives, and advised county people on solutions to problems related to remodeling their houses.

It was my job to escort demonstration teams to the Iowa State Fair and stay in the 4-H girls' dormitory on the fair grounds. Until this time I had never been to the State Fair before because of its closure during World War II. I enjoyed riding the giant Ferris wheel, and viewed the famous 600 pounds of butter transformed into a perfectly sculpted cow that was annually a proud symbol of the Iowa State Fair and kept behind glass inside a refrigerated room at 40 degrees.

Two weeks of vacation time each year was included in my appointment to Bremer County, but the only time I was not required to be present for work in an adult or youth program was in the winter months. I rode Union Pacific's City of Portland streamliner from Iowa to Ketchum, Idaho, and took skiing lessons at Sun Valley two years.

Each year the Iowa State Legislature met, a bill was submitted to remove the Iowa Farm Bureau county funds that provided the office and expense account for Iowa county agents. My second year I worked in Bremer County the bill passed successfully and in that county I no longer had an office or money to operate programs. I decided to look into the Oregon Extension Service I learned about from an Oregon agent when I attended the National Home Demonstration Agents Convention in Chicago earlier that same year.

I accepted an Extension Service position with a Federal appointment at Oregon State University that gave me a salary boost and provided a state owned automobile for my work. In Iowa I had to own an automobile for my work and drove over 20,000 miles a year on the job. In Oregon, all extension agents had full faculty status whereas in Iowa they were only employees and not a part of the faculty.

The last month of my position in Bremer County I received many dinner invitations from 4-H leaders and women's group chairmen. I went to a different home every evening and learned what my leadership had meant to their programs. A county-wide farewell for me was organized the last week before the end of my contract on July 1. I was feted by a large attendance for a potluck dinner at the meeting hall in the center of the county, and they presented me a farewell gift of expensive luggage that I used later for many years.

I moved to the Pacific Northwest, a distance of 2,000 miles from my Iowa home, and my work for the Oregon State Extension Service began as agent-at-large to travel around the state of Oregon, much larger than the state of Iowa. The agricultural agent, my co-worker in Bremer County, Iowa, eventually moved to the state of Washington in a similar position.

At the Oregon State International Club I met Yesh Pal Puri, an agricultural doctoral student from India. He requested a visit to my Iowa farm when he learned I was going there for Christmas. He wanted to see and learn about Midwestern farming, and he traveled with me by train to my Iowa home. My father liked him and spend days talking with him, a relief from a time of grieving the death of his father, my grandfather, that happened the day after the student from India and I arrived in Iowa.

A Different World

A student from India learning about the Iowa farm corn crop.

When an opening developed in Marion County, Oregon, the largest county staff of the Oregon Extension Service, I was given that position and immediately appointed by Oregon's State 4-H Leader to write the new to-be-published 4-H project bulletins in home economics.

I supervised the placement of International Farm Youth Exchangees from foreign countries in homes in Marion County during the two week period of the Oregon State Fair, and placed several in Marion County homes for longer periods of time. An exchangee from the Netherlands had an extended stay in Marion County and later, after marrying her husband in Holland, immigrated to USA and chose Oregon for their home. They invited me to their USA citizenship ceremony and reception in Portland, an interesting outcome of my professional international work.

I began research about Citizenship Development in the 4-H program for the National 4-H Foundation, Washington, D.C., and I studied the application of learning theories in the 4-H program of Marion County, Oregon. A two year research project measured the effectiveness of application of learning in the specific area of citizenship, and incorporated many methods of theory application.

The Chemeketans are a Salem outdoor club that I joined, and participated in several weekend hikes. The last weekend in May I climbed Mt. Hood, 11, 249 ft., with their climbing team that began the season each year on that Cascade Range peak. I was the only one on the climb that had not previously climbed a mountain. We started out at 2 a.m. in the moonlight, and stopped to eat breakfast at the 10,000 ft. level while keeping warm sitting beside hot steam vents. The goal was to reach the summit before noon when temperatures increase and made the snow slippery. We were successful.

On the return down, at 10,000 feet on the mountain, the men took me off the climbing rope and left me alone to return by myself to Timberline Lodge at 5,000 feet. I watched the men run down the mountain side, and I slowly and painfully walked down the steep mountain pulling each foot up in turn out of the deep snow on the descent. That afternoon I finally walked exhausted into Timberline Lodge, and drove my car to return to my Salem apartment.

I skied a third winter at Sun Valley Idaho with a Marion County Oregon Extension Service coworker and we also camped at Crater Lake National Park and Yosemite National Park. She became a lifelong friend, and all through the years we continued to enjoy dinners together.

It was my job to escort Marion County 4-H members to Oregon's 4-H Forestry Camp in June, and to teach a class there the first year of my work in the state. At the camp I

A Different World

was introduced to Kenneth Palen, a teacher of 4-H forestry. The intensive program did not make time possible for any other communication. When I returned to my Salem office my co-worker asked me if I had met Ken Palen, and "yes" was all I could say.

The three day July 4th holiday I traveled with the Chemeketans to camp at Diamond Lake and to climb Mt. Thielsen, a Cascade Range rock pinnacle 9,194 ft. high. From the top I had my first view of Crater Lake on a beautiful clear day.

Glaciers eroded Mt. Thielsen, the extinct volcano, over the millenniums creating a uniquely narrow spire on top. To get to the top of the narrow pinnacle no climbing tool could be used for support on the vertical spire above sheer cliffs that drop 2,000 feet into the valley below. I took deep breaths to pull myself up the final eighty foot spire. It was necessary to pull my weight higher arm by arm. It was shaky for me, and I had to change arms quickly to make it to the top. Going back down was a problem as I frequently had to quickly shift my weight to my left arm. My right arm did not have collarbone support, therefore, it could not support my weight and it was dangerous for me to climb a pinnacle using only my arms. I realized the danger I was in on the Mt. Thielsen climb and it put fear in me to never again climb another mountain.

That summer my co-worker asked me to take over for him at the Marion County Fair to meet the agricultural judges and handle their assignments. Ken Palen reported to me for his 4-H Forestry judging assignment, and I gave him his folder of work. He reported back to me to check out at completion of his assignment. I noticed the bald spot on the back of his head and judged him to be a married man as he was well mannered, business like, and did not initiate friendly conversation.

Later that summer, I was invited by an extension agent I became acquainted with in Iowa, also hired as an Oregon extension agent in the Hillsboro office, to drive to her apartment after work on a Friday afternoon to arrive in time for the evening meal. When I arrived her table was beautifully set with black square glass plates I will never forget; art and entertaining her specialty. Sitting at the table was Ken Palen. She started to introduce us and we interrupted to tell her we had already met. She and Ken had desks in the same office in Hillsboro's Washington County Courthouse. I do not remember anything else about that evening except the food was excellent, and as hostess she was outstanding in leading conversation as she was an active Toastmistress Club member.

In September, I received a phone call from that same Hillsboro extension agent friend asking if I was interested in going to the football game between Oregon State University and Stanford University. If Oregon State won the game, they would play in the Rose Bowl in Pasadena January 1. Ken Palen planned to go to the Stanford game, and she had made arrangements to ride with him to Corvallis where she had a boyfriend who was also going. If I would go, they would stop in Salem to pick me up. I agreed to go.

Ken Palen drove his new Ford station wagon to Salem and they picked me up. We stopped in Corvallis to meet the girl's friend who had a Cadillac that he preferred to drive to Stanford. He also had another girlfriend waiting in his car who was known to me as she was an Oregon State extension specialist that I had met at earlier meetings on the campus.

It was a long, many-hour drive to Stanford to the football game. Three wanted to sit together in the front seat which left Ken Palen and me to sit in the back seat. We listened to the front seat conversation and became acquainted as we shared amusement at front seat hilarious conversation moments.

Oregon State won the football game against Stanford University. After the game there was a prearranged meeting at a Palo Alto restaurant with the brother of the Corvallis man, a dentist who owned an airplane at the San Francisco airport. When we were finished eating, the Corvallis man's brother asked if we would like to fly over San Francisco at night to see the city lights. We thought that a great idea and drove to the airport for a magnificent flight with him as pilot over Golden Gate Bridge and around the city on a clear and beautiful evening. We would never forget that flight.

That evening did not end with the flight over the city lights. After the flight we went to the Purple Onion, a cellar club located on Columbia Avenue in the North Beach area of San Francisco. A popular music and nightclub for entertainment, it gave us more time for acquaintance before time to finally check into a motel for the night. The next morning we had to start out early for the twelve hour return drive to Oregon.

In January, Ken Palen phoned and invited me to have dinner with him at a well-known Italian restaurant on Portland's Skyline Road. I drove there after work on a Friday afternoon and met him. The view of Portland from the restaurant was beautiful, and it was the beginning of future dates when he drove to Salem to meet me.

That year I was recognized by the U.S. Department of Agriculture and given an award as part of a unit for superior service for meritorious leadership in stimulating participation of county people in aggressive and successful extension programs.

My summer vacation was planned with a co-worker, and a friend from Iowa State student days who was living in the state of Washington, to drive to Crater Lake National

Park where we three camped overnight before driving to Yosemite National Park. We camped in Yosemite for a week and hiked to the top of Yosemite Falls, and hiked and sunbathed on the top of Vernal Falls, and viewed the Yosemite Valley from Inspiration Point 6,603 feet.

I discovered the interesting history of John Muir and purchased four etchings: *Yosemite Falls*, *Bridal Veil Falls*, *El Capitan*, and *Three Brothers Peak*. I put them in matching frames, and they have hung on a wall of my bedroom all through the years. One of those evenings in Yosemite Valley, while lying in my sleeping bag and enjoying the lovely weather, I made a decision that if Ken Palen ever asked me to marry him, I would accept his proposal.

In September, a year after getting acquainted on a weekend drive to the Stanford and Oregon State football game, Ken Palen drove to Salem to take me to an Oregon State University football game in Portland's Multnomah Stadium. After the game he drove to Crown Point, the highest point in the city of Portland, and stopped to show me the lights of the city. It was the first time I had been there to see the lights of the city from that vantage point. While admiring the scenery together, Ken proposed to me and I said, "Yes." That evening we became engaged.

CHAPTER 6
Marriage

Ken and I were married in a Portland church by the pastor of Hillsboro's Calvary Church, a mission congregation without a building where Ken had been baptized and confirmed. We lived in his apartment in Hillsboro until he purchased a newly built house on Delsey Road N.E. in the new Arrington addition of the city. A World War II veteran, Ken was eligible for an Oregon State Veterans Loan. The house was built by a new contractor in Oregon, and when finished he lived in it during the holidays. He left all the curtain rods and curtains for us.

My husband went to work immediately putting in the lawn around our new home. He laid drainage ditches on all four sides of the house that was built in what had been a filbert orchard. Several of his office mates, Washington County agricultural extension agents, helped him with the yard work including digging a well in the backyard for irrigation, laying out garden space, pouring a cement patio in the backyard, cementing a sidewalk around the house and on the driveway into the garage.

Our Hillsboro home.

We accompanied the Best Man at our wedding, and his wife, to ride the ferry across the Columbia River to the state of Washington to dig razor clams. It was my first clamming experience, and cleaning them was an initiation. In the years that followed, we took family and friends who visited us to experience razor clam digging, and it was always an enjoyable time together.

Ken made an appointment for me with his dentist, and my teeth were found in good condition, but the dentist said I should not have crooked upper front teeth. He capped them to be permanently straight. I have always been thankful for that change, and wished it could have been done in my earlier years.

My husband was thirty-one years of age and anxious to become a parent and his mother never quit talking about wanting grandchildren as all of her friends had them. She told people at our wedding she was anxious for a grandchild. It embarrassed me to have my new mother-in-law talking about it at our wedding which caused guests to look at me to see if I looked pregnant.

In June of the following year, I gave birth to a premature baby girl and the doctor said it was then not known how to save babies with underdeveloped lungs. Birth control pills were not known and not in use at that time and many babies were born that were not wanted, therefore, medical science did not devote research to how to save babies. The doctor's religion was the same as ours, and he suggested calling our pastor to baptize the child immediately. The pastor arrived within minutes for the baptism.

I received a phone call from an Oregon State Extension Service supervisor requesting my interest in a work assignment in Yamhill County to fill a vacancy of an extension agent going on a sabbatical leave for a year. I accepted the position July 1, and daily commuted from our Hillsboro home to the Yamhill County Extension Office.

The next year, on a February morning, when I had just completed a home visit request to advise a homemaker in need of advice about her remodeling project, I was on return to my office in a state owned auto and I was stopped by a flagman at the bridge over the Yamhill River. A portable home in need of the entire width of the bridge was on the opposite side of the bridge approach. The flagman guided me to park on the bridge approach to ensure enough room for the house as it crossed the bridge. I watched the house moving across the bridge until the flagman began wildly flailing his arms at a car coming over the hill on the highway behind me.

I looked up into my auto mirror to see the side of a car and realized instantly the car would hit me, and at that second I felt the impact. I grabbed the steering wheel with all my strength as my car went over the bridge approach embankment. I knew the river had recently been at flood stage and when I wakened from unconsciousness I was lying in water on the roof top of the car. I thought I was in the river and I needed to quickly get out of the car.

Blood was running down my face from hitting the windshield on impact. My legs were under me and I could not move them. I grabbed at the illustrative material I borrowed from the Oregon State home furnishing specialist for the appointment as it had laid on the seat beside me, and I lapsed into unconsciousness.

The next thing I remember was a man's voice asking if I could stand on my left leg. I could see a little daylight, but my vision was so poor I could not see two men were lifting me, holding me up as they moved me up the steep river bank. I followed instructions and stepped on my leg, and the next thing I remember I was sitting in the front seat of a car on its way to McMinnville. The driver talked to me, but I as unable to comprehend what he was saying, or to even answer his questions.

Next, I remember lying on a gurney in the McMinnville Hospital Emergency Room, and fading in and out of consciousness. When I realized I was in the hospital I asked if "the others" were there which brought complete silence. I wondered about the people in the car that hit me.

Later, I awakened in a hospital room with my husband at my side. Nurses ran periodically in and out of the room to monitor me.

The next morning, an Oregon State trooper knocked on the doorway of my hospital room and inquired by calling my name. He said he had filed my official state accident form for me, and that he was parked on the opposite side of the bridge when he saw my official state car, with an Oregon State seal on the door, go over the bridge approach. He said it was his job to take command of any official State of Oregon car in need, so he jumped out of his car and ran across the bridge, on foot, to the opposite side to rescue whoever was inside the car. He pulled me out of the car and up the river bank, and put me in a car that transported me to the hospital, but my vision was so impaired I had not seen him.

Several days later, the McMinnville doctor released me to my Hillsboro doctor. My Hillsboro doctor allowed me to return home, but required I stay in bed for a week before returning to my Yamhill County office. I was anxious to return to work though my face had two glass cut gashes across the forehead that went all the way to my left eye, and I limped from fluid on my knee caused by the signal light on the steering wheel that punctured my left kneecap when I went over the steering wheel as the car hit the river embankment and rolled over.

It was helpful to me to return to my desk in the Yamhill County office after a week of confinement in bed, and I continued with my schedule as it had been earlier planned. I completed my year on the job before the birth of our daughter that occurred within twelve hours of my doctor's plan for my pregnancy.

The night after the birth of our daughter I was awakened in my hospital room when another patient was brought into the two-bed room. It was the next morning when I met my roommate, the wife of the vicar of Hillsboro's Episcopalian church. My daughter was born at 12 o'clock noon and their daughter was born at 12 o'clock that night. During the night I heard the vicar rejoicing over the birth of their daughter because they were so thankful it was a girl. The next day they told me they had an older daughter, and they had adopted a baby boy.

The vicar's wife was interested in knitting and discovered I knew how, and that I taught women to knit. She learned the Portland YWCA had knitting classes and convinced me to join her in attending them. The YWCA cared for children of class students, and it was perfect for our children. It was the beginning of years of friendship with our children of the same age. We kept in contact every year, even after our family moved to the Oregon coast and to the capital city of Salem. Our daughter and the their daughter, born within hours of each other in Hillsboro, both graduated from the University of Oregon in the same class.

My husband was State of Oregon service forester in Northwest Oregon years before and after our marriage. His office was in the Washington County Courthouse along with the Oregon State county extension service agents. The county agricultural extension agents became his friends and he joined in their activities, especially the Hillsboro Men's Garden Club.

The largest meal prepared for guests at our Hillsboro home was while my husband was the president of the Hillsboro Men's Garden Club. He entertained all the members and their wives at a picnic in our backyard where he barbecued chicken halves for one hundred guests on a twelve foot long, concrete block barbecue pit in the center of the patio. We furnished chicken and ten dozen rolls which disappeared rapidly. Guests brought potluck dishes. We made coffee and homemade ice cream. Several county agent friends also brought freezers full of homemade ice cream to make enough gallons to feed everyone.

I joined the Hillsboro Women's Garden Club Pioneer District No. 13, a member of Oregon Federation of Garden Clubs, affiliated with the National Council of State Garden Clubs. When I was first vice president, I developed conservationist John Muir as the theme for the year's program with quotations from him each month of the year.

My husband and I entered arrangements in Hillsboro Garden Club shows held each year and received many ribbons for our displays. The men's garden club selected the rhododendron as the official flower of Hillsboro, and we received newspaper publicity with our photos in it for our many winnings in local flower shows.

Milford Reed and family returned to our home from a U.S. State Department Pakistan/Bangladesh foreign assignment. Nancy was age nine years, and Mark, born in Pakistan, was seventeen months old. Mark was baptized in our church with my husband and me as godparents. Milford and my husband became close friends when they both had an office in the Washington County Courthouse. Milford invited my husband to become a member of the church, a mission congregation at the time, and later Milford joined the U.S. Department of State as a foreign service officer.

My husband was elected president of the church congregation and served in that capacity including delivering the sermon one Sunday when the temporary minister was unable to be there, and it was impossible to find a substitute at the last minute. Each year he traveled to the church Synod Convention. When he was a congregation officer he went to all the businesses where the church owed money, and was successful in his request they expunge the church's bills. When he was president of the congregation and attending the Synod convention, he requested, and was granted, removal of the Mission status of the Hillsboro Calvary congregation.

I was in charge of the church's weddings. It was common at that time that a bride and groom chose a new church building for their wedding even though they were not members of the church. It was my job to meet with the bride in advance and plan the wedding reception, and at the time of the wedding I spent six hours at the church setting up the reception area, supervising the reception, and cleaning up afterword. I bought a coffee and tea silver service to use at the weddings, preferred rather than having strangers come into the new church and use the facilities.

My Iowa/Oregon friend from my husband's office, married and our friendship continued over the years. She phoned me when John F. Kennedy arrived in Beaverton to campaign for the presidency, and requested I go with her to the place where he was scheduled to give a speech. We both had small daughters in our arms as we entered the area, and we were ushered into the front row. When JFK arrived he stood right in front of us to give his speech.

When our son was born we named him after his father. A short time after his birth our doctor diagnosed my aching right hip as exhausted; the result of the car accident in Yamhill County two years earlier when my left knee was punctured by the signal light on the steering wheel as the car crashed into the Yamhill River bank and rolled over. The left knee joint filled with fluid. I had a new baby to care for, and also a daughter two years old, and the doctor decided not to put me in traction to allow the healing of the exhausted hip. He devised a plan that I could walk only one hundred steps a day from the time I awakened in the master bedroom until I went to bed in the evening. The doctor had been in our home as a guest when the Reed family was with us on home leave from their State Department foreign assignment, and the doctor remembered the location of our bedroom, bathroom, hallway and kitchen.

I walked to the kitchen table after rising in the morning, and sat there all day with my husband getting the children up, making breakfast and dinner in the evening. We had a portable TV that rolled into the kitchen where the children and I watched during the day time hours. Our son's crib was on wheels next to the table beside me. During the daytime, while my husband was at work, our daughter walked to the refrigerator and sink to retrieve baby bottles of milk which she placed in warm water to heat them for feeding. I counted the steps every day and kept them to one hundred successfully. My hip was restored to health and remained healthy following the doctor's exact prescribed procedure.

The Reed family returned to our home on leave from foreign assignment in South Korea where they adopted a little girl. Their adopted daughter and our son were baptized in Hillsboro Calvary Church. Milford and Jean Reed were baptism godparents for our son, and my husband and I were baptism godparents for their adopted daughter. In August we drove to San Francisco to be there when the Reed family boarded a ship to leave again for South Korea and another State Department foreign assignment.

A destructive October Columbus Day storm that had an unusual strong jet stream pulled warm, moist air from a tropical typhoon to collide with the cold air mass off of the Oregon coast and the result was strong winds. A funnel effect intensified the winds further as the storm moved north between the Coast Range mountains and the Cascade Mountains. The roof on our home was damaged by the wind and was replaced by the insurance company. Many homes in our area sustained severe damage. A neighbor's patio roof landed on our back yard. Later, that same month, we had an earthquake while eating the evening meal. The floor began to ripple in large waves and my husband yelled "earthquake, run to the door and stand in the doorframe." The epicenter was a few miles east of us. There was no earthquake damage to our home.

Before our daughter was old enough to go to school I took both children, ages four and two, to Iowa on the *City of Portland* streamliner train in a sleeping car for the two nights travel before arrival in time for the Thanksgiving holiday. President John F. Kennedy was assassinated while we were there, a time never to be forgotten. I watched it all on my parents TV. My husband arrived December 21 on a long-delayed train that was sidetracked seven times for derailments due to twenty degree below zero weather that caused train rails to fracture in the western states.

The next July, we drove to my parents Iowa farm for a visit before a drive to Detroit, Michigan to visit the Reed family. Mrs. Reed was hospitalized during their home leave assignment from Rabat, Morocco. The Reed children and our children enjoyed playing together.

We went to Greenfield Village and toured the adjacent Henry Ford Museum in Dearborn, Michigan that holds vintage airplanes, locomotives, fire engines, boats, streetcars, guns, home furnishings, early American shops and industrial equipment. We walked past the picket-fenced buildings where once lived and worked Stephen Foster, Noah Webster, Luther Burbank, Charles Steinmetz and Henry Ford. We saw the chair from Ford's Theater in Washington, D.C., on which Lincoln was seated when he was assassinated, and we saw the Wright brothers' bicycle shop from Dayton, Ohio. We enjoyed every minute of our time at the large museum.

In August that same year, my first cousin and his bride traveled to our Hillsboro home on their honeymoon. We ferried them across the Columbia River to the state of Washington for an enjoyable time clamming and camping. They remembered their days with us many years later, even recalling the patience I had when our children colored on the hallway walls of our home just before they arrived, and they said I was very patient with the children. My years of teaching parent-child relationships involved a balance of love, limits and discipline plus the many skills a mother must possess that include teaching, interior decorating, cooking, dietetics, psychology, hygiene, social relations, clothing, household equipment, and a host of other things. All too often, a mother's many skills are overlooked so I appreciated my cousins noticing what I did when they visited in our home.

December of that year, a near-record snowfall was followed by record amounts of rain resulting in floods of the Willamette River that made it impossible for the Palen grandparents to drive from Central Point in southern Oregon to our Hillsboro home to celebrate Christmas with us. My mother arrived from Iowa by train earlier in December to care for our two children, and to run the household while I recovered from bone graft surgery to correct the problem in my right shoulder that left my right arm unsupported since my youth. My doctor discovered my unattached collarbone pieces and ordered a bone graft to correct the problem.

Two different orthopedists, recommended by my doctor, examined my collarbone problem and refused to work on it because they said the graft would be too large to be successful. I remembered the orthopedic clinic in Salem where I had my ankle treated after a skiing incident that crossed my legs in deep snow on a run between Timberline Lodge and Government Camp. I consulted the head doctor of that clinic and he examined my collarbone pieces with tears running down his cheeks when he realized his profession was to prevent anyone having to live years with an unsupported shoulder that did not grow to its normal length. He examined my teeth, measured my leg bones, and determined I did not have osteoporosis, therefore, predicted a graft would be successful. He was a graduate of the University of Iowa Medical School and asked me the name of the doctor who operated on my collarbones in my youth. He knew of the doctor and also knew that doctor was not an orthopedist.

Margaret Krug Palen

CHAPTER 7
Palen's Pacific Perch

We moved to Hobson Point on Tillamook Bay when the Oregon State Forestry Department placed my husband in charge of the North Unit of the Tillamook State Forest and in charge of timber sales. I became a Tillamook County extension agent working out of the county courthouse office on the many aspects of consumer problems.

The middle class I learned is oriented toward the future, and urban living and the present. They can picture themselves in an improved or different situation. The lower income class is oriented to the past. They identify with rural attitudes and are non-rational, have limited self-horizons and lack security. The world revolves around them as they are not socially integrated.

Tillamook County, with more miles of Pacific Ocean beach than any other Oregon county had many retired people living inexpensively in beach housing. I had many challenges in my work in Tillamook County that made a difference in people's lives when they participated in my programs.

The USA government yearly family cost of living reports came across my desk, and I recall one that was how much it costs to raise a child to age eighteen. The cost was different in the different regions of the country, and in 1970 in the Western part of the United States it cost $25,000; however, total cost per year to raise a child generally rises as the child grows. Cost in the child's eighteenth year can be as much as thirty to forty-five percent higher than in the child's first year. The increase is sharpest in clothing and food.

Our home was high above Highway 101 with a wide view of Tillamook Bay and the city of Garibaldi and we called it our "Pacific Perch." We loved our home on Hobson Point that had at one time been the home of the person in charge of the Garibaldi Coast Guard Station. I painted a picture of it and the beautiful view that included Garibaldi.

Pacific home painting by Margaret Palen.

Our son started to Kindergarten and our daughter to second grade at Garibaldi Grade School. My husband was elected to the Neahakanie School Board during the years we lived there, and he was elected president of the board, the largest school district in the state of Oregon.

In our first year of residence on Tillamook Bay, the Reed family returned on home leave from foreign assignment in Kenya, and arrived in Portland to rent a car and drive to our Bay City home on the Pacific Coast. It was a joyous time during the Thanksgiving holiday. Milford Reed carved the turkey for our Thanksgiving dinner. The children all had a great time together playing on the nearby coastal sandy beaches.

My assistant professorship with Oregon State University included a month of vacation each year, and at Christmas we flew to Disneyland and stayed all week to see the New Year's Rose Parade and we went to the Rose Bowl football game.

Northwest counties, Clatsop and Columbia were included in my work in addition to Tillamook County. My extension agent federal appointment included the development and teaching of courses on applied color to adult students. Basic to my instruction was the creation of a good learning environment since my courses contained technical information applied to a variety of fields. I taught in Tillamook, Clatsop, and Columbia Counties in informal classroom situations which demanded an extensive use of an organized learning environment. I incorporated many methods into my workshop format to insure effective learning for the students. My supervisor commended me for my teaching, and I received tenure three years after returning to work as an Oregon State extension agent.

A continuing part of my teaching included nutrition in family life. A workshop project asked the women to write their ideas of nutrition in family life. Here are some examples of what they wrote:

"Nutrition is an important factor in family life – proper nourishment means a healthier and happier family.

Without learning the food values of family diets, and the diet needs of each member it is hard to plan the right meals."

"If a person knows about nutrition your home life will be better."

"Nutrition is very important in family life as we need well balanced diet to be happy and healthy."

"Proper nutrition in family life provides a feeling of well being. When properly planned, one is without the hunger feelings that lead to snacks of sweets, etc. Nutritionally balanced meals are particularly important for growing children to avoid listlessness and alertness in school."

"Protein is important as a body builder. Green leafy vegetables are important for vitamins."

I organized township extension education groups for women that grew in interest and attendance that continued many years after I no longer worked as an Oregon State University extension agent. One of the group chairmen kept me informed for many years about their activities, and it was years before she wrote me their group no longer existed for lack of members. She wrote, "I miss our group."

One year we drove to St. Paul, Minnesota, where the Reed family was living while Milford was a graduate student at University of Minnesota in international economics. My husband and I were given the privilege of taking their oldest daughter to the University of Minnesota to enroll her as a freshman student.

Another year we drove 3,000 miles across USA when I had a month vacation and my husband had as much vacation time from his many years of service with the State of Oregon Forestry Department. Along the way we visited my family in Iowa, and drove on to Washington, D.C., to the Reed family home that was in Alexandria, Virginia. My husband transported the contents of Milford's bank safety deposit box to him that had been in safe keeping in Oregon all the years they were on U.S. Embassy assignments in Pakistan/Bangladesh, South Korea, Morocco, Kenya, Liberia, and Vietnam. While at their home we toured the major historic sites and museums of the Washington, D.C., area and Williamsburg.

Christmas Day, when our children were eight years and ten years old, we flew to Honolulu, Hawaii. We stayed at the Royal Hawaiian Hotel and especially liked their Christmas Day luau. Hawaiian Airline had a $5.00 special to fly to the major islands, and we traveled to Maui where we saw silversword for the first time, then to Kauai, and to the Big Island of Hawaii.

Visiting Hawaii with the children.

Visiting Hawaii with the children and grandchildren in 1994.

A Different World

Then next Christmas our family of four traveled by train from Portland to Gardiner, Montana, where we were met by a Yellowstone National Park bus that drove us to Mammoth Hotel for Christmas Day celebration followed by snowcat tours into the park to see Old Faithful Geyser erupt in twenty degree below zero weather, and another day by snowcat to see Yellowstone Falls where we were allowed to only be out of the snowcat for five minutes in the twenty degree below zero weather. We stayed in Mammoth Hotel a week and participated in the New Year's Eve park employees' celebration.

Visiting Old Faithful Geyser, Yellowstone National Park.

Margaret Krug Palen

A Different World

CHAPTER 8
Oregon's Capital City

The Oregon State Forestry Department promoted my husband and we relocated to the state capital city. We moved to Salem after purchasing a home about two miles from the Oregon State Capitol building.

Coast Range mountain views are always spectacular from our Salem home. A short distance on the street east we see Mt. Hood's tall, snow-covered peak and Mt. Jefferson, the second-tallest peak in Oregon.

Salem is a delightful place to live. It is the center of one of the most fertile valleys in the world. The city is also at the hub of one of the most diverse recreational areas in the world. In a little more than an hour from Salem, it is possible to be at the Pacific Ocean listening to breakers and savoring all the delights of a marine environment. In just more than an hour in the other direction, one can climb high mountain trails and tramp through snow well into spring and summer. North an hour is Portland, a major metropolitan area with all the cultural attractions, and south about the same direction two major universities offer intellectual and cultural challenges. Salem is a governmental power center, the hub of state government, and a county seat. The high rate of volunteerism, the success of charities and churches, and a healthy community spirit all reinforce Salem as a pleasant place to live. Salem's climate is salubrious.

The first Christmas after we moved to Salem our children were young and we went to Victoria, British

Columbia, to the Empress Hotel's three-day Christmas celebration. We drove from Salem to Port Angeles, Washington, to catch the ferry across to Victoria only to find the winter ferry schedule changed to only one ferry a day, which we had missed. We drove to the Port Angeles Airport and chartered a plane to fly the short distance to Victoria, and carried "Santa's bag" along with our suitcases.

The four days at the Empress Hotel were joyful for our family and started with the first all-day organized activities for children. My husband and I bought a small Christmas tree and decorated it for our children's hotel room. Christmas Eve was an elaborate dinner and we joined another family that had two children, and later sat in the lobby to enjoy the Christmas Yule log program that evening. Santa Claus came that night to our children's room.

Christmas Day we continued to eat with the same family, and enjoyed the activities planned by the hotel to celebrate the holiday including a Yule log ceremony that evening. December 26th is Boxing Day in Canada and special meals were served. We visited the Olde England Inn where we had stayed in the honeymoon suite right after our marriage, and also visited the English replicas of Anne Hathaway's thatched cottage and Old World garden, and William Shakespeare's birthplace. When it was time to leave Victoria we caught the ferry to Port Angeles, and returned home to Salem.

When our son finished his requirements to become an Eagle Boy Scout he applied to be a delegate to the International Boy Scout World Jamboree in Lillehammer, Norway. He was fourteen years old, the youngest age for a delegate, when he was interviewed and chosen to go to the Jamboree. After he departed early for a week home-visit in Finland, we received a phone call from the National USA Boy Scout office in New Jersey asking if our son could receive his Eagle rank in Lillehammer at a ceremony for USA scouts eligible for the award. My husband answered the phone call and gave his permission for our son to receive his Eagle rank at the Norway World Jamboree.

The more I thought about our son receiving his Eagle rank in Norway, the more disappointed I was because mothers were always present to pin the Eagle award on their son. I remembered our son's correspondence before he left for Europe included information about the national Boy Scout office chartered flight to the Jamboree. I applied for a passport for myself when I sent in my son's application for his passport because I wanted to travel to Europe, and evidently had a premonition that it would be sooner rather than later. I phoned the Boy Scout national office and inquired if they had an empty seat on their chartered plane so I could go with them and see my son receive his Eagle rank. They had one seat in the last row of the plane. I made arrangements with my Iowa parents that upon returning from Europe I would fly from JFK Airport, New York to Iowa, to be there for their 50th wedding anniversary celebration.

Copenhagen was the first place where the USA chartered Boy Scout plane landed in Europe. The gray color drabness of European airports, the lack of colored advertising, was my first impression of Europe. The quietness of Europe impressed me—stores closed at noon on Saturday and all stores were closed on Sunday. We explored the city I had known only as being the capital of Denmark, and for Hans Christian Andersen stories. I was so excited just to be in Europe that I wakened early the first morning, and exited the hotel to walk the nearby streets. A California passenger on the same chartered plane was also up early on the streets due to the time zone difference.

At lunch the first day in Copenhagen, I learned firsthand about Danish open-faced sandwiches. I also saw the little mermaid statue in the harbor, and it remained a long time in my memory. I never forgot the 16th and 17th century architecture spires of the city.

The outside views of Christiansborg Palace, and the last night at Tivoli Gardens would be repeated again in my later years. This first time in Denmark the tour bus stopped in the countryside where we saw topless bathers on the beaches. This was unfamiliar to us, and the local guide with us requested that we not stare at them.

It was my first time in Sweden when we went to Uppsala where I visited the Lutheran Cathedral that is a larger architectural structure designed like the small church where I worshiped during my early years. We went to the Uppsala cemetery to the grave of former United Nations Secretary-General Dag Hammarskjold. I remembered his death in an African airplane crash. In Sweden I learned about Axel Munthe and Selma Largerlof, authors who achieved world-wide renown.

In Stockholm I went on my first guided tour of a Royal Palace. I especially remember the royal crowns on display. The Swedish guide suggested we stop in a grocery store to see all the frozen prepared foods that, at that time, were unknown in USA grocery stores. Members on my Boy Scout tour went for walks from our hotel to see the street vending machines selling condoms, not seen in USA at that time.

I was excited to see the country of Norway. Before going to the International Boy Scout Jamboree we toured Bergen, an old Viking settlement, and learned about the Hanseatic League's trading empire in 14th to 16th centuries. We drove to Troldhaugen, the home of Edvard Grieg, Norway's most famous composer, and walked the grounds, and saw where he is entombed.

A Different World

In Oslo I saw a 12th century wooden stave church and discovered they have a smoke house smell. I bought a miniature wood replica stave church to remember the occasion. We saw the nude sculptures in Oslo's Frogner Park, and I learned they attract man's desire and search to know intimately!

The second time I was in Norway we boarded the coastal steamer at Bergen for an unforgettable trip covering a distance of Norway's coastline which has no equal in Europe. It was a visit to the Land of the Midnight Sun. Going to North Cape, the "Top of Europe," was exciting. We rode several ferries to reach this northernmost point in Europe that is one of the great natural wonders of the world. A ferry took us from Honningsvåg to North Cape in forty-five minutes. The first "tourist" to reach North Cape was in 1664 although its history begins in 1553. Judging from the number of tourists that were there, the world has changed to make this a popular and reachable adventure.

We were only allowed one day at the International Boy Scout Jamboree. I was awakened early that morning by a mother on the tour that was assigned to escort me to find my son at the Jamboree. We met him on a nearby trail where he was returning to his campground from an overnight camp-out with Scouts from other countries. That afternoon I was escorted to the stage of the USA scout center and seated with the USA Boy Scout executives to represent the mothers of the boys receiving their Eagle Award at the ceremony. I pinned my son's Eagle award on him.

Margaret Krug Palen

Gets Eagle (LILLEHAMMER, Norway) Dick Palen of Salem, Ore., receives Eagle Scout Badge from his mother, Mrs. Kenneth Palen, during award ceremony at 14th Boy Scout World Jamboree here.

Scouts Win Eagles

LILLEHAMMER, Norway — Twenty-seven American Scouts received the top badge rank in U.S. Scouting at Nordjamb '75 — the 14th Boy Scout World Jamboree here.

Among them was Dick Palen, son of Mr. and Mrs. Kenneth Palen, 2665 Alvarado Terrace S, Salem, Ore.

And on hand to pin on the badge was Dick's mother, Margaret.

The ceremony was held at the campsite of the U.S. Scout contingent to this world Scouting event, which some 2,500 U.S. Scouts and leaders attended the first week of August.

Newspaper story of Richard's Boy Scout Eagle Award.

A Different World

My husband and our daughter had never traveled in Europe. My husband booked a twenty-two day tour that included five countries in Europe—England, France, Switzerland, Italy and Spain. England was the first country my husband wanted to see because of his Palen heritage. He had always been told his genealogy began in England.

I kept a diary of our family travel together in Europe. The first thing upon arrival in London, with our two jeans-clad teenagers, was check-in at the St. James Hotel, close to Buckingham Palace. Both children had favorite Britannia brand jeans and they were familiar with the British flag on them, however, they had never seen a real British flag until they saw one flying in London. We exchanged USA dollars for British pounds and immediately walked the short distance to Buckingham Palace for our first views of it.

The Albert Pub Victoria Carving Room was where we had our first meal in England, and we ate traditional English roast beef and Yorkshire pudding with English trifle dessert. I carried a flight-bag size electric automatic percolator in my luggage, and in our room I made freeze-dried coffee and instant hot chocolate for the children. That evening we walked to Victoria Station and the Victoria Theater area where there were many people on the streets. We instantly really liked London!

The next day, we toured Westminster Abbey and saw the "stone of scone" and the coronation chair. We watched "the changing of the guard" at Buckingham Palace. We took a taxi to the Tower of London to see the "Star of India" diamond that is beautiful beyond belief! The gold coronation garments in the Crown Jewel rooms were amazing!

We shopped "where the Queen shops," at Harrods. That evening we rode in a taxi to the Phoenix Theater; we had tickets given to us by our tour hostess to see the comedy,

The Unvarnished Truth. We sat in the "dress circle" and enjoyed the play.

The London telephone directory listed a London fireman with the same name as my husband. We phoned his home and his mother answered our phone call. The next day she traveled by bus to meet us.

The third day in London we hailed a taxi to the British Museum. Large crowds were arriving and we headed immediately to the Egyptian exhibit to see the mummies. I wrote a list of what we saw in the Egyptian Gallery. I always remember seeing the famous Rosetta Stone that unlocked the secret of Egyptian hieroglyphics and was so amazed to see how small it is! We searched the King's Library, and looked at the Wycliffe Bible translated from the Latin Vulgate. We saw many handwritten manuscripts of Bach, Beethoven, and also Handel's earliest edition of "Messiah." We looked at the yellowed-with-age Magna Carta.

The Portland Vase and Elgin Marble fragments of the Parthenon in Greece were memorable, and they enlarged our comprehension of what man has done and what man can do. The British Museum contains so many artifacts from other civilizations that it made me aware of the British dominion over the world at a time when history was collectible.

We went to Trafalgar Square that is named after the Battle of Trafalgar where the English fleet defeated the French. Then we went to Piccadilly Circus, and also took photos of the Parliament Building and Big Ben.

The last day in London, my husband and son went to the British War Museum while my daughter and I went to St. Paul's Cathedral for the morning communion service. It was a short walk from there to Government House, St. Catherine's House at Kingsbury and Aldwych, to research Palen and my maternal Tanner family genealogy. Records began in 1837, the first year of Queen Victoria's reign.

A Different World

"Palin" was the only name we could find, and there was no spelling of that surname with an "e" in it. We consulted with the person in charge of genealogy about our family, always saying there was a county in England many years ago named Pale, and the Palen name derived from that county. We were told we should search for Palen in Ireland where there was an area named "Pale." There was never a county of that name in England. We began years of Palen genealogy research after that realization.

My daughter and I walked to the National Gallery to see the famous Jan Van Eyck paintings, and then went to the bus stop for Kensington Palace. The statue of Queen Victoria outside the palace shows her at age eighteen as it was where she was living at the time of her ascension to the throne. We toured the room where she was born, and also where she was a princess.

We traveled by "tube" to the Victoria and Albert Museum. Their reign imprint on the city is noticeable. That afternoon we rode the "tube" to Piccadilly Circus to meet my husband and son at Fortum & Mason department store for pastries and tea. Close by is the Wedgwood store and I went to see London prices of my turquoise Florentine pattern. I bought a Queen Elizabeth II Silver Jubilee plate commemorating her twenty-five years on the throne while my husband and son shopped for fishing flies, and they rode a ferry across the Thames River to the H.M.S. *Belfast* to tour the ship.

It was inexpensive to get around in London. Four people traveled as cheap as one in London taxis. "Tube" and double-decked bus stations and stops were easy to locate. There was free admission to all British museums that had the concept of preserving culture. There was no language barrier, only idiomatic, metaphoric expressions to learn. In later years, we traveled to London five more times, but did not repeat any of the sites we saw on this first time in the city.

A thirty-five minute flight from London to Charles de Galle Airport in Paris gave us a four day stay in that city. Our first site was the fantastic modern mushroom effect and glass tubes of the airport. A bus transported us through the gray, colorless city to our Hotel Cayre' on the left bank described as Bohemian chic. I loved our turquoise room with white furniture.

We immediately read a Paris map and started to walk to the Eiffel Tower. The map was small in scale and we did not realize the great distance to the tower, and should have taken the subway entrance just outside of our hotel. It was late and raining when we finally arrived at the Eiffel Tower and we only rode to the second level where we ate our evening meal at the bistro.

It was still raining the next day when a bus picked us up for a tour of Paris. We immediately went again to the 1889 Eiffel Tower. The guide pointed out the bullet holes on the mall across from the Eiffel Tower in the building that was occupied by Nazis during World War II. My husband went to the top of the Eiffel Tower the next day and took photos of the city.

We went on a guided tour of the 170-foot Arc de Triumph built in the time of Louis de Philip. A World War I unknown soldier is buried there with an eternal flame. The tour bus drove us past the U.N.E.S.C.O. Palace, the Monsart Dome of Napoleon Bonaparte I tomb, and gold statue of Joan of Arc.

The tour bus left us off at the Louvre Art Gallery where we headed for the lunch area. Our children used their International Student Pass card for half fare. The statue of Venus de Milo and two statues by Michelangelo, the Winged Victory statue, and one of Leonardo de Vinci, the famous portrait of Mona Lisa behind "bullet-proof" glass remained in my memory. I first learned about the beautiful flower gardens in Fleur de Leis pattern in front of the Louvre from my architecture professor when I was a student at Iowa State.

Paris is a city of little shops and small store fronts. There are many iron-work balconies like in USA's New Orleans French Quarter. Our Paris tour drove past the bookstalls, animals and plants along the Seine River. We saw a Henry IV statue on an island in the Seine River. We had a view of the Palace of Justice and San Chapelle, finished in 1248. We stopped at Notre Dame Cathedral, called "Our Lady," started in 1163 and finished in 1250 A.D. We had a twenty-five minute tour of the cathedral and noticed the flying buttresses, and the gargoyles that put water from the church roof back into the street. The 12th and 13th century rose windows: red/blue Old Testament; rose window blue/green New Testament are lovely.

We drove to the left bank Latin Quarter student district—Sorbonne location. The tour guide said since 1610 all books and courses have been changed from Latin into French.

Place de la Concorde was on the tour where we saw an Egyptian obelisk for the first time. It was beautiful with gilded hieroglyphics that made them obvious. My husband noticed all the London plane trees that are so common in Paris.

After the tour our son found his way along the river banks where men were fishing in the Seine to watch and take photos. My husband and our daughter went shopping and rode the subway system. I went on an art tour of the Louvre that lasted one and one-half hours. We all met back at the hotel.

The third day in Paris we went on a tour of the Palace of Versailles and to Fontainebleau. My forestry husband noticed hawthorn and locust trees that lined the freeway all the way from Paris to Versailles. The gardens of the Palace of Versailles are very beautiful. I remembered my architecture professor at Iowa State showed slide photos of those gardens in our class. We toured twenty of the 2,000 rooms in the Palace of Versailles.

After lunch, we drove to Fontainebleau. We stopped at the home of Rousseau and his art school where Millet and Corot studied. The Palace of Fontainebleau is French Renaissance and filled with ornate frescoes, and the actual furniture from Napoleon's time is still in the rooms. The Egyptian influence in furniture was strong during the Napoleon era.

That evening my husband and I took the Metro to the Montmartre district, and hiked the rest of the way to see the Sacré-Cœur. We entered the church and listened to organ music. It is the highest point in the city of Paris and people congregate there at night to look at the city lights. There were so many people! The dome on the Sacré-Cœur is the design copied for the U.S. Capital dome in Washington, D.C. We returned to our hotel at midnight after walking many miles, and going partway by subway.

The last day in Paris our family went by Metro to the dock for a boat ride on the Seine. It was a beautiful day; excellent for photography, and spectacular views of Paris. We sat on the top deck and loved it. We walked along the streets from the boat dock and saw shops of designers Givinchy, Balencia, and Nina Ricci on the way to return to the Arch de Triumph. My husband went to the top of the Eiffel Tower and took more photos of the city. My daughter and I spent the afternoon shopping at Printemps where we ate lunch in a garden on the 6th floor. Then we walked to Galeries Lafayette department store in the next block from Printemps department store.

A Different World

At 7 p.m. our family had reservations for a Bateaux-Mouches dinner-at-night on the Seine River. We rode the Metro to the boat landing for the cruise. We had a lovely time and delicious food. We drank four year old Champagne to start the dinner, and five year old wine with the meal. I ate foie gras (liver pate) for appetizer and quail for main entree. Our daughter ate lobster for appetizer and duck for entree. My husband and son ate frog legs for appetizer. Our son had Guinea hen for entree, my husband had Chateaubriand Bearnaise steak for entree. Dessert was Roue de Brie cheese and flaming Baked Alaska.

In later years I returned to Paris seven more times, but never had time to repeat the activities I did on this first tour with my family.

The hotel desk wakened our family at 4 a.m. to leave for the airport and an 8 a.m. flight aboard Air France to Geneva, Switzerland. Breakfast served aboard was more than we could eat on a forty-five minute flight. Due to the time zone change we arrived in Geneva at 8 a.m. to an empty airport. It had been a long time since we had seen so few people!

The famous Jet d' Eau in Geneva rises four hundred feet high and was the first thing we saw. It is the trademark of the city and it is lovely. Geneva means: "coming out of water."

We immediately went on a guided tour of the city and learned Lake Leman is the largest alpine lake in Europe. The Rhone River divides the city of Geneva. There are two-hundred-fifty United Nation Organizations in the city of Geneva. One third of the city is made up of gardens and parks. The floral clock in the city is unique and it always keeps perfect time. The flowers all over the city were beautiful!

We saw the 1865 Russian Orthodox Church with six spires of twenty-two karat gold leaf. Tourists are not allowed to go inside; it is only for members.

The Geneva Opera House is a small reproduction of the opera house in Paris.

We saw the statues on a 1918 International Reformation Wall: John Knox and students of Calvin. They were made by the same sculptor that made the statue of Christ in the harbor at Rio de Janeiro, Brazil. One side of the plaque has Luther and Zwingle's name. Since 1815 the city is officially neutral. We learned that Geneva is the cultural center of French-speaking Switzerland.

We saw the Red Cross and World Health Organization headquarters buildings. Geneva is also the Capital of World Scouting.

After the tour our family went on a walking and shopping tour in "Old Town." Our son bought a Swiss Army knife that does "everything." Then we went to Les Armures restaurant and ordered a cheese fondue Swiss specialty that is delicious. Bing Crosby records were playing in the restaurant.

The next morning was Sunday, and we slept until 8 a.m. in our small hotel rooms where the beds folded out of the wall. Our children were tired of continental breakfasts—croissants and hard rolls, jam and coffee.

We walked to St. Pierre (St. Peter) Cathedral where we saw Calvin's chair dated 1535. The cathedral was in restoration and the inside torn out. We saw vaulted burial tunnels below the floor. The cathedral was a significant Protestant cathedral following the Reformation when it was the "Rome of Protestantism" in Europe.

We walked around the beach areas to see the London plane trees by the water and in the parks. Our daughter and others on the city tour found a beach where they paid to go in and where there were many topless bathers.

Evening meal was pizza in San Marco's open-hearth fire oven. We watched it baking and discovered the black olives had pits in them. There was not as much meat and cheese on them as there is on American pizza. We returned to our hotel for a quiet evening of listening to radio, reading and went to bed early.

The next morning was Monday and it was raining again. A bus was arranged to pick us up at the hotel lobby and take us to the *Star of Geneva* boat cruise on Lake Leman. It rained and rained! We had a blanket to wrap around us; alpine air is chilly. The homes around the lake shore are beautiful. We saw where Lenin lived, and where Eisenhower lived when he was in Geneva. We returned to the hotel at noon. It was still raining.

That afternoon we walked the streets and saw newspaper headlines: Pope Paul est mort (is dead). He died of a heart attack during the night. Years earlier I said that if I ever would go to Rome, the Pope would be dead. Now it was true as we next were going to Rome.

My daughter and I went shopping at the Bucherer store, famous for Swiss watches, and they gave us each a demitasse spoon. I bought a seventeen-jewel Bucherer ball watch for $31 USA. Our daughter bought a sterling silver charm, a beautiful "cock-co-do clock" with weights for $20 USA. My husband joined us to finish shopping. He had been to the bakery for pastries. The rain continued and we could not continue walking the streets. Dinner was at the closest restaurant to the hotel. We ordered escargot, a first time for us to eat snails. They were delicious!

We traveled other cities of Switzerland six different times in later years, but never again toured in Geneva. The rain showers continued the next day. We boarded a bus for the airport to fly on Iranian Airlines to Rome. Stewardesses gave us English newspapers to read while waiting for lunch to be served. It was a little over an hour flight and we lost one hour of time in the zone change between Switzerland and Rome. We enjoyed good views of Italy and the coastline before circling and landing at Leonardo da Vinci Airport. We flew over Vatican City with our first view of it from the air.

The weather in Rome was dry, sunny, Mediterranean-like, and it felt wonderful! Italy is the size of California. A Rome tour hostess met us at the airport and gave us an introduction to the city on the way to Hotel Fleming. Lasagna dinner was served in the hotel dining room.

A beautiful sunrise awakened us the next morning. Continental breakfast with Cappuccino coffee awaited us in the hotel dining room. Then we had an 8:30 a.m. bus pick-up for a city tour of ancient Rome's narrow streets—all very old! There were no subways in Rome. The guide explained the archaeology and art of the city. Streets were very quiet as Romans were on vacation in August. The city was also mourning the death of Pope Paul. His funeral was scheduled for Saturday.

There was a shortage of coins in Italy at that time, and bargaining was done so people would buy more merchandise. Our guide suggested talking with your hands if language is not known. The city of Rome was bankrupt, and could not water anything so everything was dried up and the streets were not clean. Rome park statues had "junk" hanging on them. It added "age" to everything that was already very old.

The local guide explained the "She Wolf" symbol of Rome. It is children being suckled by a wolf. The bridge with that symbol was built in Mussolini's era.

A Different World

We drove past the 1960 Stadium of Olympic Village, and then drove to Piazza del Popolo where Roman tiers are images of "old Rome." At the 1735 Baroque style Trevi Fountain we all threw coins in to wish to return to Rome. The guide said we could write to the city for a refund if we did not return; however, we did return and I also returned several additional times in later years.

The Column of Marcus Aurelius, 2nd century A.D. is beautiful! It pictures victories and battles he won against the Barbarians. It was one of my favorite sites in Rome.

There are thirteen Egyptian obelisks in Rome that were brought to the city in the time of the Caesar Augustus reign. All the obelisks have Christian crosses attached to the top to convert the pagan idea of them. Four fountains also date to Caesar Augustus' time. We enjoyed viewing them.

We arrived at the 137 Spanish Steps built in 1700's that are really French and Italian. We walked up them to the Church of Holy Trinity at the top of the steps.

Then we drove to the Coliseum, the Flavian Amphitheater, which means two theaters together. The construction shows a double theater. The statue of Nero on the front was so colossus that the people of Rome called it a Coliseum. The white marble on it disappeared in the Middle Ages; it was used to build palaces and churches. The Roman numerals above the arches are still visible. The prophecy of the Coliseum: "As long as it stands so will the seat of Rome; when the seat of Rome disappears the world will disappear." The remains of barracks of gladiators are across the street from the Coliseum. Our children watched the wild cats in the Coliseum.

The Arch of Constantine is an ancient monument in Rome. It is located on the grounds of the Coliseum along the road taken by triumphal processions in those days. It was erected about 316 A.D. to commemorate the triumph of

Constantine I, after his victory over the rival Emperor Maxentius at the battle of the Milvian Bridge in 312 A.D. It is the largest of three such arches which survive in Rome. The central arch of the Arch of Constantine is about thirty-five feet high and about twenty feet wide. On each side are two arches about twenty-five feet high and fifteen feet wide. The entire structure is about sixty-five feet high and about eighty feet wide and is covered in white marble. There are eight detached Corinthian columns, four on each side which stand on plinths on the sides of the archways. The inscription: "Constantine overcame his enemies by divine inspiration." He was the first Roman emperor to become a Christian.

The Roman Forum, civic center of ancient Rome, has remains of three styles of columns still standing: Doric (oldest style), Ionic, and Corinthian (youngest style with acanthus leaves). A composite column had acanthus leaves and Doric combination. We also looked at the remains of the Temple Venus located on top of the hill by the Forum.

The 1911 memorial to the first King of Italy, Victor Emmanuel II, has two chariots and two winged victory statues on top of a huge white building, and I recognized that it frequently appears in articles written about Rome

I was excited to walk in the Pantheon, the most important building in Roman engineering according to my Iowa State University architecture professor. It is perfection in architecture. Pantheon means "all Gods" in Greek; built in 27 B.C. by Marcus Agrippa, reconstruction by Roman Emperor Hadrian. Niches are where there were pagan gods, and now they have paintings. The dome is a perfect circle 135 ft. high and 135 ft. wide. The "oculus" at top is a circle open to the sky. There are no windows in the building. Light volcanic stones were used in the center of the dome. The coffered ceiling recedes in four steps that were of interest to me from my Iowa State professors' explanation. The roof was originally supported by bronze, but now has wooden support. The bronze supports were melted down and used in making the canopy of St. Peter's Basilica. The 1,800 year old doors are the original bronze doors.

    The Vatican was the last part of our Rome tour. It is said to be the least populated city in Europe with only 840 people. We walked in St. Peter's Square designed 400 years ago with statues of bishops, cardinals, popes, and saints that surround the top of the square.

    St. Peter's Basilica was crowded with preparations for the funeral of Pope Paul. We saw the building of the bier for Pope Paul's body to lie in state. The dome of St. Peter's is four hundred feet high. Then we walked to a nearby pasta shop on a restaurant street for lunch and returned in the afternoon to see more of St. Peter's Basilica.

    I was surprised to be able to view the body of the Pope at the time of World War I lying under glass beneath the altar of one of the side chapels. Mosaics in St. Peter's were made by the Vatican Art School. The mosaics are made of very beautiful pieces that are so tiny they look like oil paintings from a short distance. The sculptured statues in St. Peter's did not fit the niches in my way of thinking. They are all reaching out of the spaces to impose feelings on nearby people and evoke emotions of those passing by them. I felt they were out of scale for the area. Under the main altar is the tomb of St. Peter and only Popes can say mass there.

    We viewed "The Pieta" through bullet-proof glass. Christ is too small in scale and Madonna is huge in comparison to give proper significance, but I did not like those proportions. Photos often do not show size difference due to the angle of photography.

We walked to the Sistine Chapel that was the highlight of the Vatican tour. It was fantastic to see Michelangelo's paintings from 1508–1512 that I had studied in my university art classes.

The Vatican Museum was viewed last. We saw third to fourth century A.D. Roman copies of Greek sculpture and I looked at Pope Leo's coat. Popes, except for Pope John, have all been from aristocratic Italian families.

Red, pink, yellow and white oleander was in bloom all over the city of Rome, and it added lovely color to all the ruins. Our hotel had huge urns of blooming oleander.

We caught up our laundry that evening and it dried fast in the warm Rome weather. The next morning, after breakfast, our tour bus left at 7:10 a.m. for Naples, third largest city in Italy. It was a beautiful drive among olive trees, tobacco fields, and vineyards among poplar trees. We saw 4,000 ft. high Mt. Vesuvius and it looks like Oregon's Mt. St. Helens though it does not have snow on it.

The Bay of Naples was beautiful on our way to the harbor to await a boat ride at the docks. We took a hydrofoil thirty-five minute ride to the island of Capri from Naples. The tide was high so we were unable to go into the Blue Grotto.

The Isle of Capri is beautiful; bougainvillea and morning glories blooming everywhere. It was Roman Emperor Tiberius' favorite vacation place. Anacapri is the city on the Isle. It was crowded with people. We rode a bus to Hotel San Michele, on the high point of the Isle, for lunch. We saw the home of famous Swedish Dr. Axel Munthe. His restored gardens and his home are filled with treasures of his time in Tiberius.

Returning to the city center we took a funicular railway to the harbor and caught a twenty minute hydrofoil ride to Sorrento, a beautiful city with orange trees and lemon

A Different World

trees that had fruit on them. We shopped at a store that sells embroidery, laces, and inlaid woodwork. I bought an embroidered linen handkerchief. My husband bought, and had shipped to Oregon, a set of six tables for our living room that had Roman designs made of cherry wood inlaid with fruitwood.

We stopped at Pompeii to see what we could of the ruins before its closing time. We saw a World War II pillbox tank along the side of the highway, a remnant of World War II. We stopped at a Cameo factory and watched the artisans carving cameos in the work rooms that were beautiful and expensive. Our evening meal was at Abbey of Monte Cassino, original home of the St. Benedictine Order. After eating, it was a one and one-half hour drive to our Rome hotel and we arrived at a late hour.

The next morning, we ate a continental breakfast before a walk to the bus stop to ride to downtown Rome. We climbed the Spanish Steps for a view of the city, then walked to the Column of Marcus Aurelius and to the Roman Forum for photos. We gave our son the map of Rome and he found and led us everywhere we wanted to go. After lunch, we walked to Christ-In-Chains Church to see Michelangelo's statue of Moses. I was amazed at the height of that statute!

We window-shopped as we walked back to the bus stop to return to our hotel. That evening we again walked to the bus stop and rode downtown to see the city at night. We walked to Vatican City to find everything dark and locked. We window-shopped and boarded the bus at Piazza del Popolo for a late hour return to our hotel.

After breakfast the next day, a bus picked us up at 7:10 a.m. to drive one hundred eighty miles on "Motorway of the Sun" to Florence in northern Italy. We passed many olive trees and hill-towns along the way. We learned Etruscan history, and about Etruscan towns built on volcanic rocks with Roman aqueducts, olive groves and vineyards. We took a Cappuccino coffee break before the last hour of drive to Florence.

We saw the old wall around the city as we approached Florence. The first view of Florence was from a viewpoint balcony that had a replica of Michelangelo's *David* statue in metal that had aged to a green color. Roofs of orange colored tile made up the city view, and the dome of the cathedral.

We drove to the third largest cathedral in the world—Basilica of St. Mary's of the Flower, built of three colors of marble: green, red and white, to represent the Holy Trinity. Beautiful! Inside we saw Michelangelo's last Pieta that he started for his own tomb, and chiseled his self-portrait in the body of Nicodemus holding Christ—"Deposition From The Cross." A pupil finished the left figure when Michelangelo died before he completed it. There were three more unfinished Michelangelo figures to view that he never completed for his tomb.

In Florence we visited the Florence Baptistery, and listened to a lecture about the twenty-one centuries old bronze doors that are on the oldest building in the city. We looked at Giotto's famous leaning Bell Tower. Then we walked to the Academia Gallery to see the famous fourteen-foot high *David* statue by Michelangelo, and his other unfinished sculpture pieces. He was twenty-one years old when he carved *David*, and it took him two years to complete it. I noticed *David*'s hand on the right side is too large in proportion to the body. This statue was in the city square by the city hall until a falling stone broke the left arm. The statue was then moved into the city museum. The wooden tree-like stump by the statue's right leg gives it more base needed for balance. Veins in the statue's neck and "Adam's apple" are important details to notice the realism.

The head is "Greek" in style, the body Roman, and the actual Biblical David was a circumcised Jew.

Next, we went to the crowded Galleria degli Uffizi to see paintings by Giotto, Da Vinci, Botticelli, and Michelangelo's 1507 *Holy Family* painted on wood set in a round frame. I liked the *Birth of Venus* by Botticelli, and remembered studying about it in my university art history classes in my undergraduate major field.

After lunch at Piazza near the Basilica of Santa Croce (Holy Cross), we visited tombs of Michelangelo, Dante, Galileo and Rossini (Barber of Seville). Our son helped me in a shop by the square, close to the church steps, by bargaining for a small statue of David. I promised him it would belong to him in the future. Mass was in progress in the church for the funeral of Pope Paul in Rome and there were many people around the church.

We saw a third *David* statue in Florence. It is the same size as the original statue and it is a copy located in front of the city hall where the original *David* statue stood before being moved to the Accademia Gallery.

Evening dinner was in the city of Orvieto, a city famous for lace and an Etruscan hilltop town built on volcanic rock, surrounded by olive orchards and vineyards. We visited the beautiful Orvieto Cathedral before dinner. Mass was in progress for the funeral of Pope Paul and the street was filled with people on benches lining the buildings in the lovely summer evening. Orvieto Cathedral is older, at 1290 A.D., than some that we viewed. Horizontal stripes on Orvieto's Cathedral gave a black and white effect with mosaic frescoes on the front facade in the beautiful summer evenings.

A delicious Italian lasagna meal followed our tour of a very old 13th and 14th century wine cave. We descended a long steep stairway down to see the wine casks that were white with mold and cobwebs, and the temperature was noticeably cool. We had a late 10 p.m. return to Fleming Hotel in Rome.

The last day in Rome, after breakfast, we moved our luggage to a hotel storage room. We rode a city bus to Piazza del Popolo and caught a bus to the Coliseum, then transferred to another bus to walk the Appian Way to the Catacombs.

We walked to St. Sebastian Church to tour the Catacombs and see Christian church history. The word *catacombs* means: "Christian Center." At St. Sebastian the Catacombs are seven miles long. We were shown only a small section of the underground cemetery for the first Christians. Fish and dove symbols are important in the Catacombs. Oil lamps hung from the ceilings.

We returned to the Colosseum area and ate lunch at a sidewalk cafe in the block next to the Colosseum. A bus returned us to Piazza del Popolo. My husband and I walked to a large park area to botanical gardens and zoological area of the Borghese Gallery. All galleries were closed because it was Sunday. Many of the stone statue busts were mutilated and the park in decay due to the city's bankruptcy. Fortunately, we traveled again to Rome in later years when Italy was again financially stable, and the parks and the streets were manicured and repaired.

We had an evening departure to Leonardo da Vinci Airport. We boarded an Argentina Airlines 747 jet for a two hours and forty-five minute flight to Madrid, Spain. We checked into the Agumar Hotel at 2 a.m. It had a lovely marble floored lobby, tapestries on walls, and crystal chandeliers; a beautiful hotel. We went to bed immediately to awaken for a continental breakfast and a short-distance walk down the street to find a bank to exchange money. We then walked to the Prado Museum, and our children used their International Student Passes to get in for half fare admission. We followed a self-tour guide.

We took an afternoon tour through the main streets of the city of Madrid, a capital of four million Spaniards. Spain is a socialist country. Madrid is 2,000 feet above sea level. The tour included the Royal Palace and Chalet of Villa where the king lives. The Royal Palace was built in the 18th century by Charles III. The king, at the time we were there, did not live in the palace.

We learned what caudillo means: "one whose power and will make everything right in the Spanish-speaking country; one who sets himself up as a dictator."

It was the hottest part of the day and we went to the 365 acre Parque del Buen Retiro. A mounted statue of King Alfonso is impressive. People were boating on the lake to keep cool. Shops were closed during the hot time of the day when they take afternoon siestas, around 3 p.m. to 4 p.m., and shops open later into the evening. Madrid does not have a spring season, only winter into summer season.

The fountains in the center of the city of Madrid are beautiful. The Neptune fountain is 18th century. The Dolphin fountain is my favorite. We went to interesting Columbus Square.

Madrid has many London plane, locust, eucalyptus, horse chestnut, and twinberry trees.

A tour guide took us to the Prado Museum, considered by many one of finest in the world. I looked at more paintings studied in my *Art through the Ages* Iowa State University text book. Velazquez, Rubens, El Greco, and Goya's *The Clothed Maja* and *The Nude Maja* were interesting.

The tour guide left us off in the heart of the city (movie district) for shopping at the end of the city tour. We found an air-conditioned restaurant where we ate cold watermelon and drank lemonade, then we took a taxi to our hotel. We went on an evening bus ride from our hotel for an hour to make a full circle of the fountains lighted at night that are very beautiful.

The next day, we had continental breakfast in the hotel before taking a taxi to El Rastro Open-air Flea Market where our tour guide recommended we haggle over prices. Bullfight posters were a bargain. A donkey with a straw load of pottery was the most interesting site in the market. My daughter Susan and I bargained for a Moroccan tooled leather purse, and purchased it for her.

After lunch in the hotel dining room we rode a circle bus and got off four times to take photos of fountains, especially the dolphin fountain. This was a Spanish religious holiday and there was a bullfight, otherwise they are held on Sundays. We took a 4 p.m. guided tour to the bullfight. It was interesting and a worthwhile first experience. I could hardly make it through the first killing of the first bull. More bull killings were not quite so difficult to watch, but still left me feeling for the helplessness of the bulls. Knowing that it is actually a slaughtering ritual helped me understand what was happening.

The girls from New York City on our tour bus could not take it when the second bull was killed, and they left the stadium to return to the hotel. Our two children stayed through it all. The bullfight started at 6:30 p.m. and was over at 8:30 p.m. There was a brief intermission after the first three bulls were killed. The most acclaimed matador was handsome in a white costume decorated in silver and gold—absolutely beautiful! He cut off the ear of the bull and carried it around the stadium to receive an ovation.

After the bullfight, we went to dinner in our hotel dining room and enjoyed Spain's national dish Paella. The basic ingredient is rice. It was delicious! It combined seafood, poultry, vegetables, and small clams in the shell that we ate with the house wine. After dinner we made more coffee in our hotel room.

The hotel's continental breakfast the next morning served Melba toast that was a welcome menu change. It was our last full day in Spain. We taxied after breakfast to El Corte Ingles department store where our daughter bought a pair of Spanish dancing dolls. All four of us met later in the day in that department store and returned on the same bus to the hotel.

The guide made reservations for us to hear gypsy guitars and see Flamenco dancers "in an atmosphere of Spanish gaiety" and our last fling in Europe on this tour. We took a taxi to Torres Bermejas nightclub to see the Flamenco Show. We had a front row reserved table next to the stage, best seats in the house, and watched the one and one-half hour floor show. Passionate guitars joined the dancers' castanets in a fiery flamenco show. It was interesting to hear the loud rhythmic noises they made with their hands clapping in time to the music and to the sounds of the castanets. Costumes were black and turquoise with white, red and polka dots.

The next morning our two children slept in and skipped the continental breakfast. We watched women using feather dusters dust and dust!! Our luggage had to be in the hall by 10:30 a.m. Our bus left the hotel for the Madrid airport just before noon and our flight to return to New York.

Margaret Krug Palen

CHAPTER 9
This Changing World

I retired from work with the State of Oregon Department of Human Services Division where I was in charge of the adoption desk that required computer skills. My learning to use a computer at the Salem Public Library had made my hiring for that job possible.

When the day arrived to take our daughter to the University of Oregon for her freshman year I didn't know how I would get along without her—her smile, her pleasantness, her artistic talents shown in her embroidery work and sewing skills. Her absence was even more difficult when it was time for our son to leave home for his freshmen year at Oregon State University.

Our daughter was a student at the University of Oregon and a member of Delta Delta Delta sorority when a Nordstrom store was built in Salem. Her sorority sisters bought their clothes from Nordstrom and each year, before fall term began, we drove to Portland to the Nordstrom store to buy her wardrobe. As soon as the Nordstrom store opened in Salem I applied for a job even though I had a full-time job with the State of Oregon. I knew the Nordstrom store would hire me when I included on my application that I studied merchandising in my university major field degree.

I accepted Nordstrom part-time work on weekends, evenings and for their special sales days when I took vacation from my State of Oregon job. For fifteen years I worked in their Salem store marking down clothing, transferring clothes to other Nordstrom stores, sweeping the stock room, restocking racks, sorting sizes on racks on the floor, and filling in where they needed help in different departments. I bought all our family clothing, including clothes for the grandchildren, and my travel wardrobe using my Nordstrom employee discount.

In the evenings I also worked cleaning Truit Bros. Cannery and earned extra money to put in my daughter's student bank account at the University of Oregon. I remembered what it was like to be a college student with not enough money; therefore, I made sure my daughter had a bank account and enough money in it at all times.

Willamette University in Salem held "An Old English Christmas Dinner" and we went and took our two children. It began with the prayer of King Henry VIII and with the lighting of the Christmas candle, a wassail toast, and boar's head procession. We especially enjoyed the strolling carolers and Madrigal Singers, and the heralding of the serving of the flaming plum pudding. It reminded us of our travel together several years earlier in England.

While our daughter was a student at the University of London in England, Mt. St. Helens erupted and spread ash up to five inches in parts of Washington State. Ash landed on our house in Salem, and I collected several bottles of it that remain on our office desk.

Our daughter wrote letters home about going to the Isle of Wight, the English Channel, and to Greenwich, where the world's time is officially kept. She studied with an Oregon State University professor and a professor from the University of Washington, both visiting professors at the University of London. Her University of London credits counted toward her degree from the University of Oregon. While she was a student in London she was a guest of London fireman Kenneth Palen, in his home in London and

A Different World

he gave her a tour of the pubs of the city. She completed her term at London's university and traveled to Wesel, Germany to be a guest of our friend Ursula Schonborn at Gut Isselhorst.

Our daughter went to Italy and took the ferry across to Greece and was photographed in front of the Parthenon. Ursula arrived in Oregon to visit us in time to help celebrate our daughter's twenty-first birthday.

The Reed family came to visit us at our Salem home after Milford retired from the U.S. State Department, and they had moved to Luray, Virginia. Before retirement, Milford was responsible for the U.S. Agency for International Development's operations in the Far East. For his work in securing peace between Israel, Egypt and Jordan following the Yom Kippur War, he was given the U.S. Department of State's Superior Honor Award.

We celebrated our 25th wedding anniversary in a service at St. Mark's Church followed by a reception with the congregation. My parents came from Iowa for the celebration. The minister that married us participated in the anniversary service and, with his wife, attended the luncheon we served at our home. Mrs. Lynn, a friend from the years we lived in Tillamook County, helped prepare the meal and entertained us by whistling the tunes while she played them on the piano. Everyone enjoyed her unique entertainment.

Ken and Margaret Palen's twenty-fifth anniversary.

Our daughter graduated from the University of Oregon with a degree in health education and a teaching certificate. Openings for teachers were scarce. She was hired by the principal, where she had been a student, to teach for a year to fill a vacancy of a teacher on sabbatical leave. After that first year of teaching she became a full time student at Western Oregon State College. She lived at home and commuted daily in the car she purchased with earnings from her first year of teaching. She upgraded her teaching certificate to teach physical education, and later completed a master's degree.

Our son graduated with a bachelor's degree magna cum laude from Oregon State University. Teaching positions were difficult to obtain and he lived at home and commuted to Western Oregon College of Education to complete teaching credentials, and later a master's degree.

A Different World

The year we bought our first computer, I published my first book, *Genealogical Research Guide to Germany*. Then I published a new edition, *Genealogical Guide to Tracing Ancestors in Germany* with a cover picture of the Löhlbach church where my ancestors were baptized, confirmed, and married. That edition continued to sell many years. I published the first edition of *German Settlers of Iowa, Their Descendants and European Ancestors*, and updated it with a second edition at the turn of the century, followed by another updating a decade later with a third edition.

While visiting my Iowa family, my father's first cousin, also my high school friend two years older than me, requested to see me. She was the mother of six children and was accompanied by her youngest son when she arrived at my parents' home to visit with me. Mother disappeared, leaving us alone as she knew time together was limited. Phyllis glowed as she reminisced about the time the two of us were roommates in a Waterloo, Iowa, hotel while attending a church youth convention. She remembered we stayed up all night talking, and that she inquired about my religious beliefs, and I witnessed to her the entrance of the Holy Spirit in my life and about my saving faith through the grace of God. Happiness filled the room as Phyllis related how she also now had experienced the Holy Spirit in her life and knew she was saved by the grace of God. We embraced and shared our feelings as we conversed until it was time for her departure. We walked from the house to her car, and said "goodbye" without any feelings of sadness. Phyllis died of cancer six months later.

I have learned that I live in an invitingly big country—some 2,777 miles from sea to shining sea. I visited all fifty USA states with my parents and husband. When I began going to other countries I learned that the world keeps changing, and I discovered in other countries one's mind is engaged in learning their history, and it broadens and stretches perspectives so that a global outlook can be gained about art, food, and many facets of living. I learned that in returning to a country again there are always changes that add dimension to my understanding of the world.

In my youth, the "Seven Wonders of the World" were what I hoped one day to experience: Egypt's Great Pyramids, India's Taj Mahal, USA's Grand Canyon, the Panama Canal, New York's Empire State Building, Rome's St. Peter's Basilica, China's Great Wall. In my early years I waded in the Pacific Ocean, and stepped across the Mississippi River in northern Minnesota, but I would never have believed that in later years I would not only go to all those "wonders of the world" but would experience all the continents of the world.

Germany was a desire of mine to see from a young age when I heard my paternal Grandpa tell my mother, who was collecting family genealogy, the name of our native village Löhlbach that he said was located in the middle of Germany between two large rivers, and our family emigrated to the middle of America to Iowa between two large rivers— the Mississippi River and the Missouri River.

After moving to Salem, Oregon I met a pastor that told me about his plans to take a tour group to Germany to see the famous Oberammergau Passion Play's 350th year performance. I told him about my lifelong desire to go to Germany, the home of my ancestors, and he suggested I help him fill his tour bus. He explained if I found passengers for him I would receive a free tour for every five passengers I booked, and if I found enough my husband would also be free on the tour.

I immediately began asking everyone I knew, and I booked twenty-four people to have free tours for my husband, myself and our daughter. We made arrangements that my husband and I would go earlier to Germany, before the tour, and visit my heritage villages. Our daughter escorted our tour group to the Frankfurt Airport where we met them.

In finding passengers for a tour to Germany I was noticed by many who knew us though organizations of our membership. In April of that year, I was requested to give a "Ladies Program" at the Salem Elks Club. A monthly publication of our church had an item "Join Lutheran Tours. Call Margaret and Ken Palen for choice of time and dates. Emphasis will be on Luther Lands—Eisenach, Erfurt, Eisleben, Wittenberg, Worms—500th Anniversary of Martin Luther, and religious areas of interest."

When my Grandpa talked about our home in Löhlbach, Germany it was the only time he talked in the English language. He remembered the exact mailing address of the village, and mother wrote it down. I asked her for it, and that made it possible for me to confirm plans to go to my ancestral village. German genealogy had not been published in America at the time, and most genealogy experts attributed it to the effects of World War I and World War II, which caused persons of German ancestry to hide their cultural identity. My father's family, even in my lifetime, has not pronounced their surname correctly. It is a common word in the German language and they do not want to be identified as German.

I never gave up the idea of researching my heritage in Germany, remembering what Abraham Lincoln (1809–1865) said, "Determine that the thing can and shall be done, and then we shall find the way." My dream to go to Germany finally came true.

Ursula Schonborn, niece of a German janitorial couple in our Hillsboro, Oregon, church, first came to us to visit the grave of her uncle and aunt. I was requested to write to her father when her uncle died, and the correspondence that followed from her father invited us to Germany so he could show us the country; however, Ursula's father died before we could take up his offer. Ursula stayed with us when she came to see her family graves, and she helped me research my Löhlbach genealogy. She went with us to the villages in Germany and translated for us because the people living there did not speak English. She then guided us by map to many places in Germany she said her father wanted us to see. She read our maps and interpreted road signs. Eventually, we were in Bavaria to see the Oberammergau Passion Play with her before it was time to meet our tour group, led by our daughter; the second time for us to see the 350th anniversary year performance.

My husband and I landed in Amsterdam, considered the best preserved 17th century European city. I did not realize at the time that Amsterdam would become the European city I would most often visit because their airport was where I transferred to other places in Europe, and to Africa, and to India. Amsterdam is a huge port, and on the first visit we took a canal boat ride to see the houses on the canals built in the 1600's of black oak wood from Germany and we rented a car to visit our foreign exchange students at their family's home in Rotterdam. They took us all over their small country and showed us many windmills, museums, and everything of interest along the way.

My husband drove a rental car from Amsterdam on the autobahn in Germany to Wesel to our friend Ursula's home. She sat in the front seat of the car and read the highway signs on the way to Löhlbach, and she interpreted for us because we do not speak German, and the villagers we met did not speak English.

A Different World

When I met the pastor of the Löhlbach church I asked about research of my family in the record books that were kept in the church basement. Besides Löhlbach, I needed to trace Battenhausen, Halgehausen, Altenhaina, Dainrode, Allendorf and other villages where my ancestors lived. Eventually, years later, it led to finding two of my fourth cousins: one still living in Löhlbach and one living in nearby Huddingen.

We stayed four days in a hotel in Löhlbach, the village of my paternal ancestors, including a weekend so I could attend church on Sunday where my immigrant ancestors were married December 25, 1835. I was given the opportunity to speak to the congregation during the service according to the pastor's plan that it was a "homecoming service." I was the first descendant to return to Löhlbach of the six families that left the village in the 18th century and immigrated to America.

The opening hymn sung by the Löhlbach church congregation for my "homecoming service" was from Psalm 84:

    Mein Leben ist ein Pilgrim stand,
    My life is a pilgrimage,

    ich reise nach dem Vaterland,
    I am traveling to the Fatherland,

    nach dem Jerusalem, das droben,
    to Jerusalem, which God himself has

    Gott selbst als eine feste Stadt,
    established above as a firm city,

    auf Bundesblut gegrundet hat; da
    on the blood of the Christians that

werd ich meinen Gott stets loben.
band together. There I will praise

Mein Leben ist ein Pilgrim stand,
God himself. My life is a pilgrimage,

ich reise nach dem Vaterland.
I travel to the Fatherland.

Second hymn of the "homecoming service."

Nun danket alle Gott mit Herzen,
Now thank we all our God with heart,

und Mund and Handen. Gott
and mouth and hands. God who does

der grosse Dinge tut an uns und
great things for us everywhere, whomever

allen Enden der uns von Mutterleib
has done great things for us from

und Kinderbeinen an uzablig vill
time of birth, through childhood

zugut und nach jetzund getan.
and to the present. Has done it and still does it even now.

My German vocabulary was limited: "Ich danke Ihen, Pastor Dressler. Ich frene mich sehr, hier in Löhlbach, in der Stadt meiner Vorfahren zu Sein und in Ihnen zu sprechen."

A Different World

(Translation: Thank you Pastor Dressler. I'm very happy to be here in Löhlbach in the city of my forefathers, and to speak to you.) I then spoke in English and my accompanying German teacher Ursula translated what I said into the German language for the congregation.

I was honored at the church service and at a reception that followed it in the village auditorium. Ursula accompanied me and translated everything from German into English and vice versa because the villagers did not speak or understand the English language.

My freshman year in college I had enrolled in a German course, but at that time it was not taught by the conversational method. The entire academic year I studied German grammar, and translated difficult Goethe writings. I tried to practice what I knew in the German language with my father when I was home at holiday times, but he would not speak in the German language with me. Years later, after his uncles, his father and all his brothers were deceased he told me that he would not help me with the German language when I was a college freshman because, "It was too much bother to speak with a person who did not know the German language." Years later he spoke to me in German when he called me on the telephone, but I could not respond to him in the German language.

To learn about my German heritage, and gain perspective of my family's emigration to the "new world," I visited German villages ten different years—Löhlbach, Haina, Sehlen, Altenhaina, Battenhausen, Dainrode, Sebbeterode, Grusen, Gemunden, Herbelhausen, Mohnhausen, Allendorf, Hulgehausen, and Dankerode-on-der-Fulda. The Iron Curtain division of Germany, into East and West Germany, was still in existence at the time I began my research, and the boundary between the two areas was within thirty miles of my native villages.

A member of the Löhlbach congregation was permitted by the pastor of the church to take the church record books to his home to search for my family genealogy with the use of the immigrant information my father provided. The Löhlbach church has separate books each year for baptisms, confirmations, marriages, deaths, and there are no indexes, only items listed in the order each event occurred. I learned the church books hand writing was in old ink that was made from acorns and was dark in color that contrasted with the yellowed pages of the old books and made it possible to read the oldest German language writing. Many hours and days and years were required to trace Krug, Michel, Happel, Moller (Moeller in USA), and Paar, who are all my related families.

I visited my ancestral homes: the home where Great-Great-Grandfather Krug and Great-Grandfather Krug were born in Löhlbach, the home where my Great-Great-Grandfather Happel was born in Altenhaina, the home of Great-Great Grandma Happel in Löhlbach, the home where Great-Great Grandma Krug was born in Löhlbach, and the home of my paternal Werning ancestors in Dankerode-on-der-Fulda.

It was a short distance to Dankerode-on-der-Fulda, not far from the East German border at that time, to the village of my Werning ancestors. The Werning home is located right across the street from the Dankerode church where my ancestors were baptized, confirmed, and married. The Werning home occupant still living there was my 6th cousin, and he showed us the baptismal bowl and communion ware used by my ancestors that was still in use in the Dankerode church.

Engraved in stone along the door of the Dankerode church: Phil. 1:21 Christus ist mein Leben, Und Sterben ist mein Gewinn. (Translation: For me to live is Christ, and to

A Different World

die is gain.) In the basement of the Werning home I saw the engraved stone in the foundation with the date 1833, and Werning name of my Great-Great-Grandfather Johann who built the house.

My Great-Grandfather Happel married Jeanette Werning in America, an immigrant from Dankerode-on-the-Fulda, Germany. That search included the Brehm family that married into the Werning family in Germany, and while in the village we visited both of their original family homes.

We drove 2,245 miles between Friday, July 13th and Monday, August 6th in the car rented in Amsterdam to tour that country, then drove in Germany.

After this first visit to my heritage village of Löhlbach I returned nine more times to Germany and met my closest relatives, 4th cousins. I learned from the search of the Löhlbach records that the men in my family all were baptized Johann or Johannes which means, "God's Grace." I walked the streets of the village to find the house numbers listed in the church records where relatives were born and lived before immigration to USA. The houses with their numbers are still in existence.

We drove to Altenhaina, called Alt Heim in earlier years, to see the home built by my Happel ancestors, and where their ten children were born before emigration with their parents to America. The name of the family and date of the house construction was painted on the outside of the house.

The Pastor of the Löhlbach church drove us to Marburg, a university city of 75,000 population, where state archives hold genealogical data, and where the St. Elisabeth Cathedral holds the shrine of St. Elisabeth, the patron saint of the state of Hessen, and namesake of many of the women in my family that were born in Germany and in America.

Memories of my first year in school returned to me the first time I saw the birth home of Martin Luther in Eisleben, Germany. My first recitation, at five years of age, in front of the church congregation on October Reformation Sunday: "Luther was born November 10, 1483 in Eisleben, Germany." Mother practiced "my piece" with me over and over until I could correctly pronounce Eisleben.

Luther was baptized in the church located on the street behind his home on St. Martin's Day and given the name Martin. Each time I visited his birth home I walked to the church and visited the simple interior design of the worship and baptismal area.

I learned as a child studying Reformation history that Luther's father worked in a mine, and I supposed the family was poor, but when I visited his birth home I learned they were wealthy from a copper mine near Eisleben. The family afforded Luther an excellent education and wanted him to become a lawyer and judge. Luther was sent to Latin school in Erfurt and to Old Erfurt University. After his sudden conversion, the result of a lightning strike, he was admitted to the Augustinian Order, the highest education order of the Catholic Church at that time.

After going to Oberammergau to the 350th anniversary play, we crossed the East German border into East Germany. This was before unification of Germany occurred in 1989. East German guide Elke explained, "We prefer to be known as Germany Democratic Republic or GDR or DDR rather than East Germany as Americans know us." She translated the GDR signs that hung above highway overpasses to mean "Forward for Freedom and Socialism."

We questioned Guide Elke about the meaning of the signs across from our Erfurt hotel and she said, "This is a socialist state and not a communist state. There is no unemployment in East Germany. School children have two months of holidays. In October school children help harvest potatoes and the whole class is paid. All school children learn Russian. East Germans fifty years old and older can also learn Russian in evening schools."

Guide Elke explained, "Young people do not attend church because progress at work may suffer if they are known to be active church members. That does not mean we have no religion. It's just that we don't feel we can go to church. In a socialist baptism a child is baptized in the city hall and aunts and uncles take a vow that they will raise the child in socialist doctrine."

We looked out of the tour bus windows to view the wide expanse of cropland and fields ripe with grain awaiting harvest in East Germany. The cropland was not as neat and productive as in West Germany; however, it reminded us of the prairie country of North America with the realization it is the "breadbasket" area of Europe. We viewed large cooperative farms everywhere and the thin crops appeared as though less fertilizer is used on the land. Fields of grain were in the process of harvesting and as many as four combines worked side by side in a field; straw baling was going on in the field at the same time.

In Dresden there were murals illustrating the socialist movement that were difficult for us to understand, and they were not fully explained by our guide. GDR guides do not explain or interpret anything that would be in conflict with the American way of life or point of view.

Hotel meals in East Germany were excellent and served in multiple courses. Breakfast included pepper cheese and jagerwurst, cucumber slices, cherry tomatoes and parsley in addition to rolls, eggs, ham, sausage and cereals. Lunches on tour in East Germany cities were combinations of familiar foods and some new ones such as boiled red bell peppers cut in strips. Hotel Merkur in Leipzig served smorgasbord buffets for breakfast, the same as for the evening dinners, and the menu included caviar and truffles, fresh fruits and juices, many kinds of meat, steak and cheese, skewered meats, fried wurst, deviled eggs, caviar, Mohnkuchen (poppy seed filling) decorated cakes, cheese cakes and ice cream.

    The day of our departure from East Germany Guide Elke said, "Since you do not have an empty suitcase to carry me home with you, it is time for me to leave. Please write to me." The tour bus drove 841 miles in GDR. Our tour bus drove 1,463 miles in West Germany.

CHAPTER 10
Europe and Change in China

In 1990, when the decade performance of the Oberammergau Passion Play was given, our son and both of my sisters joined us to travel to Europe to see it. Before arrival in Germany we traveled through Spain and Portugal. It was our second time to be in Madrid. Lisbon and Portugal were interesting; places where many voyages of discovery of the Western World began. In Seville, Spain, we visited Christopher Columbus' grave and viewed the beautiful altar made from gold he found in the western world. We long remembered our Alhambra of Granada visit; the world's only medieval Arab palace in Europe, a 14th century pink castle in Spain's Andalusian region. Its fountains and lacy ornamentation are surrounded by beautiful gardens.

Historic Toledo was a memorable city. We went sightseeing in Barcelona three different years including when we were there for port stops on two of our later-year Mediterranean cruises. We saw the Christopher Columbus statue in Barcelona each time. Upon reaching Gibraltar we crossed over by ferry to Tangiers, Morocco; our first visit on the continent of Africa.

Our son had his first camel ride at Tangiers, and a tour member took a movie of his camel ride.

After seeing the Passion Play, my son and I met our German friend, Ursula, and went to Berlin to see where she had lived in her youth. We visited the Berlin Wall that had been taken down in November 1989. I picked up pieces of the wall and later framed them. Berlin seemed to us as having become an "old city with a new spirit." It was undergoing big change.

Ursula escorted us on a tour through elegant Charlottenburg Palace. Then we walked directly across the street to the Egyptian Museum where we saw the original bust of Egypt's most beautiful woman, the majestic Nefertiti! It was exciting to see it. She was surrounded by household articles and other treasures from the days of the pharaohs of Egypt that were collected by German archaeologists and preserved in the Germany museum.

While on continents of the world, other than Europe (my genealogy heritage), I learned to be careful about eating food to prevent any health problems. The first time this was very important was in going to China. To prevent diarrhea or other medical problems I learned "If you can't boil it, cook it or peel it, then forget it." In eating prepared food the same is true—if it wasn't boiled or cooked on high heat, or you could not peel it, then don't eat it! I always followed those precautions and never experienced diarrhea or health or digestive problems of any kind in going to over eighty different countries and to every continent in the world.

The year that I went to China it was often in the news with an increasing interest in people wanting to see that country. Several couples joined our plans and we flew to Tokyo and toured in Japan before flying to Hong Kong, and from there went on China Airlines to China. On the way to Japan, flying on Japan Airlines, I looked out the window of the plane we were on, and saw Japan's red circle symbol of the rising sun on the plane wings, and it sent shivers through me remembering how hated that symbol was in my youth when we were in World War II against Japan.

Eventually, I was in Japan three different years and saw the many changes in the country following World War

A Different World

II. The major sights that remain in my memory include seeing Mt. Fuji with its beautiful snow-capped peak from the window of the "bullet train" on the way to Kyoto. It is a dormant volcano that last erupted in the year 1707, with a perfectly symmetrical cone that is 12,288 feet high.

Kyoto was my destination all three different years I was in Japan. It was formerly Japan's Imperial Capital and considered the country's cultural and artistic center. Japan has more than 1,600 temples, hundreds of shrines, gardens, and historic architecture; however, many of them are very similar. I especially liked visiting Kyoto's Golden Pavilion each time I was in that city. It is set on pillars suspended over water.

I never became fond of Japanese food as I do not eat raw food, especially fish, when in foreign countries. The first time I was in Japan, we were on the way to China. The second and third times I was USA's representative to the World Lace Organization. The second time I was in Kyoto to plan the World Lace Organization Semi-Annual World Congress, and the third time I went there to attend their World Lace Congress.

Tokyo was always the first place of my arrival in Japan. It is the financial, commercial, and political capital of Japan, and the first time there I toured the amazing city that covers 840 miles. The Shinto Meiji Shrine was my first destination to tour, and after seeing it I discovered most all of the other shrines I visited in Japan looked like that first one I saw.

From Osaka, Japan, we flew to Hong Kong in order to board a China Airlines flight to Beijing. While in Hong Kong I celebrated my birthday with a reservation at a prearranged restaurant that served "flying shrimp." It was unforgettable to see the shrimp jump out of the chafing dish when Chinese wine was poured on them and flambeed, and eventually they were scooped up over and over to cook through before being served to us. The meal was a banquet with eleven courses and, as a result, I have never forgotten my Hong Kong birthday.

In China everything about their culture was a new learning experience for me. Previously it had been a land of mystery, rickshaws, pagodas, and the Great Wall. I looked forward to seeing Chinese gardens as I had only known them through the study of art. Mountains and water, I had learned, were symbols to the Chinese and how their artists gained sensitivity and visual insight. Nature had inspired them, and while in China we saw mountains in southern China that were artistic in shape, exactly like their artists portrayed them.

Memorable in China was seeing and learning about the Temple of Heaven. The top of it is a big ball representing the sun. Paradise is represented inside the building. A pair of dragons and a pair of phoenix designs on the building represent the emperor and empress. The twelve red pillars inside symbolize the twelve months of the year. In ancient days, time was divided into twelve, not twenty-four hours. The Temple of Heaven burned down in 1888 and was rebuilt in 1890.

Margaret and Ken Palen (in the foreground) visiting the Temple of Heaven in China.

I learned from our guide that in Chinese history there are hundreds of emperors. We went to the Summer Palace, a fantastic place, where we ate lunch at the "Hall of Listening Orioles." It was amazing to see and realize change happens, however slow, in China. Then we went to the Beijing Zoo to see the pandas.

Riding a bus at 8:30 a.m. the next day we started to the Great Wall, and on the way we had our first views of rural China. Many horse and mule driven carts were filled with bricks or reeds for weaving baskets. Many bicycles along the roadway, with two wheeled carts that hauled produce, replaced the old human-drawn version we thought existed in earlier years. Change was taking place!

We arrived at the Great Wall of China to find too many people there! We had one hour and ten minutes at the wall. I walked fast and climbed up on it to the next sections until I was above all the people. I wore my shorts and running shoes under my coat in anticipation of being able to "run on the Great Wall of China." I ran down the wall all the way to meet the others on our tour. That year my exercise program made it possible for me to return to what I had weighed at the age of twenty-one years.

It was a forty mile journey that day to the Great Wall, and from there to the Ming Tombs where I walked the five hundred steps down four stories below ground into five vaults. There were large jade stones alongside burial boxes to scare off evil spirits. That evening we had a Peking duck banquet. Soup was always the last course in China and at this meal it was duck bone soup, and dessert was whole apples we peeled and cored ourselves.

The next day, we went to the two-hundred-fifty acre "Forbidden City" that impressed us. Chinese emperors and

A Different World

their mandarins secluded themselves in lavish splendor there from the masses of people.

We flew from the Beijing Airport to Hohhot, the capital of Inner Mongolia. We carried toilet paper with us because of the need to squat over a slit in the ground for a toilet. We boarded a bus to the grasslands with several stops to see mud houses, and the families invited us to come inside and see their home. The women touched my hair and asked the guide how old I was, how many children I had, and about my watch and the gold wedding band I was wearing.

We saw oxen plowing in fields before our arrival at a yurt village where we moved into yurts for overnight. Meals were eaten in a dining yurt. At 7:30 p.m. we went to the largest yurt to an evening program of classical Chinese music with beautiful costumes and talented voices. They asked our group to perform and we were unprepared but we sang: "I've Been Working On The Railroad," and a two-part round: "Three Blind Mice" and "Let Me Call You Sweetheart" and closed with "God Bless America." We did not know in advance we would be asked to sing and those were the only songs we all instantly knew the words and melody to.

The next morning there was ice on the small ponds of rain water around the yurts. A bus drove us to an area to see horse racing with Mongolian ponies, camel racing, and Mongolian wrestling. I rode on a Bactrian, two humps on its back, camel.

Margaret riding a Bactrian camel.

We returned to Hohhot International Cultural Exchange Guest House (Inner Mongolia Branch) for more touring before taking a train to Beijing. The many lovely views of the Great Wall of China from the train kept us fascinated, and looking out the train windows.

In Beijing we rode a bus to Tiananmen Square where a temporary guide took us to the Mausoleum. Foreign visitors were allowed to go right in the mausoleum while the Chinese were lined up for blocks waiting to get inside. We had ten minutes to fulfill our friendship journey by paying respects in viewing Mao Tse-Tung's body lying in state under a glass dome.

The next day, we returned to the Beijing Airport to board a one hour and twenty-minute flight to Xi'an, the

A Different World

ancient capital of China and the cradle of Chinese civilization. The most significant sight there was thousands of life-sized terra cotta warriors and horses along with two life-sized bronze chariots and eight bronze horses that were found guarding the main entrance to the Qin Shi Huang Di Tomb. A 15th century bell tower in the town center also interested me.

Next, we took a two hour and twenty-five minute flight to Shanghai. A local guide with a bus waited for us and took us on a tour of the city. We stopped to tour a carpet factory and a jade and ivory carving factory; both were fascinating. That afternoon we walked through the narrow streets of Old Town Shanghai to the Yu Yuan Gardens built in 1559 A.D. We saw a 300 year old wisteria tree. One wall had five dragons on it. The guide explained the designs and the vase shaped doorways and moon gate that framed the views. This garden was familiar to me from the set of dishes I have with Yu Yuan Shanghai Garden designs. The world keeps changing, but the beauty of the gardens continues throughout all the years.

We drove to the Shanghai waterfront to see the ships, and Chinese people crowded around our bus because they wanted to practice speaking English with us. I gave them postcards that pictured the city of Portland, Oregon, and Mt. St. Helens.

The next day, our tour bus drove to a silk printing factory and to the Arts and Crafts Institute where we saw artistic demonstrations of making dough dolls, silk embroidery, porcelain etching, lantern making, silk flower craft, paper cutting, and needlepoint. That afternoon we went to the Children's Palace that is run by the government for children that pass tests for certain talents. We watched performances of ballet, accordion music, and dancing, and toured classrooms and a biology class. That evening we enjoyed a two hour acrobatic show.

The next morning, our bus drove to "the Bund" and we boarded a boat on the Huangpu River for a three hour cruise to the Yangtze River. A magician entertained us. The pilot let us ride in this cabin for good views and photos.

We stopped to see the Jade Buddha before we boarded a plane to fly two hours and fifteen minutes to Guilin. There were beautiful views from the airplane of lime mountain peaks. Guilin has a subtropical climate and humid temperatures. The first thing we saw at the airport was a huge beetle. Upon arrival at our hotel, huge butterflies, as large as my hand, were flying in the lobby. Allowing them everywhere was a change to us.

The next day, we cruised on the Li River, passed valleys and bamboo groves, through shallow waters and rapids. It was a trip filled with beautiful scenery. We saw many water buffalo, cormorants, villages, and people fishing. There were no roads or railroads along the river. This cruise was a highlight because of the natural beauty of the mountain scenery which is exactly like artists show it in their paintings. I had always thought they designed the mountains in their paintings, but on this cruise I found they painted them exactly as they are in nature.

The next morning sightseeing included seeing the Reed Flute Caves that are somewhat like the Carlsbad Caverns in New Mexico, but not the same. Then we were off to the airport for a forty-five minute flight from Guilin to Guangzhou (Canton). A local guide was waiting for us and we drove to a beautiful pagoda before going to Dr. Sun Yat-sen Memorial Hall, a circular building without posts inside.

We drove to Goat Hill to see the large granite sculpture of five goats who came down from heaven and brought rice to the people, and showed then how to plant and

A Different World

harvest it. The legend says the goats turned into rocks. The billy goat was huge; a nanny goat with suckling kid and two other goats were also on the monument, which is located on the same hill as the obelisk to Dr. Sun Yatsen. It changed the mind of Chinese people and their world to know about the goats.

We drove to Guangzhow International Restaurant for a "farewell to China dinner" that featured a large platter of Canton duck. I went with our China guide to the hotel disco, and a fun night of dancing until midnight.

Margaret Krug Palen

A Different World

CHAPTER 11
Scotland, Ireland and Retirement

I looked forward to going to Scotland, land of my maternal heritage. Edinburgh Castle, standing over Scotland's historic capital, was of great interest as it is where St. Margaret Chapel is located. I learned at a young age about Princess Margaret of England, and that she and I were both named after the saint of Scotland.

My husband is a member of the Royal Order of Scotland and their annual meeting is on July 4th. We went to Scotland one year to attend that meeting, and I accompanied him to the evening banquet. The 11th Lord Elgin, a descendant of King Robert the Bruce, was speaker at the banquet and told of the changes in Scotland's history. Two days later, we were invited to Lord Elgin's Broomhall Estate at Dunfermline in Fife. He gave us a tour of his ancestral historic home. The 7th Lord Elgin in the 1700's brought the "Elgin Marbles" and many Greek artifacts to that home. It was fascinating to see the changes made in the home to accommodate the artifacts. We were served high tea of finger sandwiches, sausage rolls, and warm scones. We were thankful for these days because we learned so much about the change in Scotland's history.

Another year on a train tour of Scotland we had more days to tour the Highlands. We enjoyed our visit of 16th century Ballindalloch Castle, the home of the lairds of Ballindalloch. It is one of the very few privately owned castles to be lived in continuously by its original family. The exact date of the origin of the castle is unknown. In the large amount of land around the castle we saw the famous herd of Ballindalloch Aberdeen-Angus cattle; founded in 1860, it is the oldest Aberdeen-Angus herd in the world. In my farm years I learned about Aberdeen-Angus cattle and this was an opportunity to learn how they have existed through the years of many changes in the world.

I went to Scotland to see the Aberdeenshire "Cradle of the Gordons" known as Huntley Castle. My maternal grandfather's family are descendants of King Malcom III via James, born in 1690, who came to America in 1724. I am in the eighth generation of that Gordon family in America. I visited the Gordon castle two different years. One year we rode a train to Huntley and walked the distance from the station to the ruined castle, the ancestral home of the chief of the Clan Gordon, Earl of Huntly. It was originally granted to Sir Adam Gordon of Huntly in the 14th century. The second time I was there, in my retirement years, some restoration was visible and several photos were made of me in the castle.

A Different World

Margaret at the Huntly Castle in Scotland.

One year in Scotland I ferried across the Sound of Iona to the Isle of Iona, birthplace of Scottish Christianity. In 563 A.D. the Irish monk Columba founded a monastery there. Iona is the burial place of Scotland's kings Duncan and Macbeth. I visited the monastery and looked at many intricate Celtic crosses in the churchyard. It was a historic and interesting experience that added perspective to understanding changes in Christianity in the world.

Returning home from these European experiences, the mail brought us an invitation from the Milford Reed children to their Luray Willow Springs farm to a surprise celebration of their parents' 45th wedding anniversary. While there they took us to Monticello, the home of President Thomas Jefferson, third president of the United States and author of the Declaration of Independence. He preferred his native Virginia and his beloved Monticello over any other place in the world. His beautiful hilltop home meant more to him than Paris, France or anyplace else in the world. He broke ground on his 5,000-acre estate in 1769, and became governor of Virginia, a congressman, USA minister to France, the US Secretary of State, and the US Vice-president; but in reference to his years of building Monticello, he was quoted as saying they were his happiest years.

The architecture of Monticello interested me, having studied architecture in college, and I learned that Jefferson was a self-taught architect preferring sixth century classical designs adhering to classical rules of balance and proportion. The Monticello dome, the first such dome incorporated into an American home, was based on drawings of the Temple of Vesta, which is located in Rome in the ancient Roman Forum that I had visited. In this changing world it is possible to view ancient architecture designs in the USA, and unnecessary to go to other continents to see them.

A Different World

In the garden of Ash Lawn-Highland (home of 5th President James Monroe, a 535-acre estate outside of Charlottesville, located only two miles from Jefferson's Monticello though totally different) we saw a 300-year-old Monroe oak tree standing tall through all the changing years.

Cruises make it possible to easily see the world in change. Before we retired we took our first Princess Cruise through the Panama Canal and we cruised through the Panama Canal two more times after retirement. We enjoyed five Mississippi River cruises aboard the *American Queen*—the largest and most opulent riverboat in the world—and immersed ourselves in Southern culture and Civil War history that changed our country. We visited Memphis, a city of musical heritage and Civil War relics, and Vicksburg and Natchez; that widened my perspective on the changing world of our country.

Three different years we were in Ireland. The first two times in Ireland we were unable to go into part of Northern Ireland because of a political conflict. The third time the conflict was resolved, and we circled the entire island. All three years we went to Belleek, to the pottery crystal centers that are in County Fermanagh, especially meaningful to me because my Scottish-American immigrant ancestor married a woman born in County Fermanagh, Ireland. I am eight generations from her, but I must have a few drops of Irish blood! I traced my Irish genealogy by writing to County Fermanagh, and they confirmed by letter that my ancestor and her father were both born citizens in that county of Ireland.

Each of the three different years in Ireland we went to Dublin to Trinity College to see the Long Room and The Book of Kells, an illuminated manuscript in Latin of the four Gospels of the New Testament believed to have been created in Ireland in 800 A.D. They are Ireland's finest national treasure. Also, all three years we enjoyed a night of food and entertainment at Jury's Irish Cabaret in Dublin. One year we were there on my birthday and it was a joyful celebration for me, to be long remembered.

We had a magnificent medieval banquet each time in Ireland at Bunratty Castle, and I realized the world has changed in the way we eat nowadays compared to that time in the world. Also, we always visited the Waterford Crystal Factory and looked at the designs and table set with the same crystal pattern I use in my home.

I cannot forget seeing the interesting cliffs of Moher in County Clare, striated limestone cliffs that reach 702 feet above the Atlantic Ocean and are always shown on programs and brochures about Ireland. They represent the world many years ago and are spectacular in today's changing world.

The Giant's Causeway, a fascinating area on the north coast of Ireland, is where it is possible, in clear weather, to look across and see Scotland.

My husband retired and wanted me to retire so we would have more time together, each having managed years of a professional life. My retirement became official the following spring. The summer of my husband's retirement we traveled to Germany and Spain, Portugal, Morocco, Switzerland, and Liechtenstein. In September, we took a Mediterranean cruise on *Royal Princess* to Barcelona, Spain; Cannes, France; Monaco; Rome and Venice Italy; Sicily; Greece; and Yugoslavia. We continued enjoying his retirement in October with a tour of all the New England states and Nova Scotia, Montreal, Quebec, and spent days in New York City that included going to the top of the Empire State Building and riding a ferry to visit to the Statue of Liberty.

A Different World

When I retired the following year, my husband was in the hospital for a week with a blood clot in his left leg and one in his lungs. He was released to a lengthy recovery at home. I had time, in addition to caring for him, and decided to phone the Portland lacemaker I met at the Oregon State Fair that summer that had offered to come to my home to teach me to make bobbin lace. She said her offer was good, and she traveled to our home and gave me six lessons of a ten lessons series. I worked the other lessons on my own according to her instructions.

Some say that people who are math and science oriented, and like to solve puzzles, also like to make lace. Science is my field and I like to solve puzzles and follow directions in patterns. Bobbin lace is my favorite of the true handmade laces. In my university undergraduate studies I leaned from my historic textiles professor that European women and their children made and sold handmade lace to support themselves before the Industrial Revolution produced inexpensive lace on machines in Nottingham, England. That was all I knew and learned about handmade lace until the first time I traveled in New Zealand.

At Queenstown, New Zealand's South Island, we stopped to eat lunch at a shopping mall. My husband went to a restaurant, but I wanted New Zealand's delicious ice cream with large chunks of fruit in it, and walked the mall looking for it when I came to a shop with a lady sitting in the doorway with a pillow on her lap. I had never before seen handmade lace being made, but I immediately realized what she was doing as she moved the wood bobbins all made from different New Zealand trees. I spent the lunch hour visiting with her about handmade lace and learned there are many lacemakers in New Zealand. We exchanged addresses.

"How far do you live from McMinnville, Oregon?" the New Zealand lacemaker inquired.

"It's a half hour drive," I replied.

I learned the New Zealand lacemaker ordered her thread for making lace from a weaving shop in McMinnville and I was unaware it existed. When I returned home I visited the shop, and saw lace pillows that were very expensive.

Eight months later, we traveled to Scandinavia and arrived in Helsinki. Overnight flights to Europe arrived early in the morning, and I was so excited just to be in Finland the first time that I walked a few blocks from our hotel and entered a large multi-market building already doing business for the day. I saw a market stand selling everything to make lace. They sold pillows like the ones I looked at in McMinnville, Oregon. In Helsinki they only cost $50 USA, and could be packaged to carry aboard an airplane. I purchased a pillow and upon arrival home wrote to the New Zealand lacemaker, and sent her money and an order for bobbins made from New Zealand trees.

Many years of lace activities began for me including twelve years representing USA on the world council of OIDFA, Organization International Bobbin and Needle Lace, officially organized in France. I was elected to the executive council and traveled to Europe three times a year to attend officer meetings. Every two years a world lace Congress is held, and in my years they were held in: Belgium, Sweden, England, Czech Republic, Greece, Japan, France and Australia.

Council meetings were held in the year between each Congress, and one that was especially meaningful to me was in Caen, France. While there for lace meetings, I went to Bayeux to see the original Bayeux Tapestry. I looked forward to seeing the tapestry I had learned about in historic textiles classes in my undergraduate years at Iowa State University.

A Different World

I rode a train the short distance from Caen to Bayeux, Normandy, to see the original tapestry exhibited at Musée de la Tapisserie de Bayeux. It is an embroidered cloth—not an actual tapestry—and consists of some fifty scenes with captions embroidered on linen made with colored woolen yarns. It is two-hundred-thirty feet long and depicts the events leading up to the Norman conquest of England when William, Duke of Normandy, killed Harold, Earl of Wessex and King of England, at the Battle of Hastings. It was especially meaningful to me as, while in England, I had earlier visited that Hastings battleground.

The survival of the Bayeux Tapestry, almost intact, over nine centuries is miraculous. It was fascinating to see its length, harmony and colors, and its exquisite workmanship. There are some fifty embroidered scenes with Latin captions. In 1729, the tapestry was rediscovered where it was displayed annually in Bayeux Cathedral. After viewing it the first time, I sat down in a chair in a corner of the room and waited for the crowd going through it to dissipate, then I went through the display a second time to closely observe the details.

The Bayeux Tapestry was commissioned by Bishop Odo, William's half-brother, and made in England in the 1070's. The end of the tapestry has been missing from time immemorial, and the last section of the embroidery has been almost completely restored. The start of the tapestry has also been restored, but to a lesser extent. I enjoyed being able to see it.

When the World Lace Congress was held in Prague, Czech Republic, I went there the year preceding it to attend council meetings and plan the program. My husband went with me the year of the Congress. The Charles 4th Bridge in Prague was memorable in that city that was for 1,000 years the home of a Czech ruler. We learned the Holy Roman

Empire ruled from Prague which is one of Europe's best preserved cities with many spires.

At the turn of the century, year 2000, I traveled a third time to Sweden to see the World Lace Congress in Lund. I had been in Germany to see the 2000 year Oberammergau Passion Play, and from Berlin I rode the train to arrive by ferry at the port city of Malmo from where it was a fifteen minute train ride to Lund. The university campus, where the Congress was held, was especially beautiful, and the city of Lund easy to negotiate. I arrived in time to set up the USA national display, and learned about the many types of Swedish lace from the extensive special exhibit on display.

I returned to England three different times after I retired. The World Lace Organization activities in England required I be there. One of the years I flew from Oregon to Minneapolis and JFK, New York, and on the way we flew over Niagara Falls. I could see the falls in clear weather from 33,000 feet. The Niagara River is very wide with many rapids in it before the falls—a lovely site.

I landed in Amsterdam in rain, and changed flights to London's Heathrow Airport. I rode a train to Nottingham where my lace friends, Amanda and Arthur, met me. They drove me to the Trent University Clifton Campus and checked me in for the international lace meetings. That evening I went with Amanda to the Lawrence Lacemakers group of thirty women meeting in a large hall that was an interesting lace experience.

My Branscombe Point lace class met the next day. I had an evening reception with world executive committee members. The next days of the council meetings we made plans for the Nottingham 2002 World Lace Congress, and the Greece 2004 World Lace Congress. We made a bus tour of the Nottingham Congress venues, and walked from the Lace

Market to Albert Hall. The last day of meetings my lace friend Amanda drove me to their home that was a half hour away in the quiet countryside. I was shown their yard, garden and fish/frog ponds, and we ate delicious Welsh cakes.

The next day we drove a big circle to national parks north of Nottingham, going first to Chatsworth, the estate of the Duke of Derbyshire, the second wealthiest duke in England. The Duke of Westminster is the wealthiest. Chatsworth has a palace, and huge fields of sheep and deer herds. Then we drove to the highest peak where views of rock walls and countryside were spectacular. We stopped at Crawford Mill for a cup of tea where the first water-powered cotton spinning mill existed, 1771–1791. That evening Amanda showed me her lace projects.

Another day we drove ninety-six miles south through six counties to the Bedford Museum. I did not need to pay an entry fee because my age was over sixty years. We looked at two floors of rooms full of Victorian furniture and glass, and examined all their lace boards. Of interest to me was the Thomas Lester Bedfordshire lace room where Bedfordshire was often combined with Maltese lace. There were many antique bone bobbins, and three antique English large round pillows full of antique bobbins that I had never seen before.

The next day, we drove north sixteen miles to Hardwick Hall and toured the old house that is now in ruins with some parts in restoration. We ate lunch in the old kitchen in the basement of the new house that had *ES* initials with crown on top in stone on all sides of the roof. We took over an hour tour of the house to see huge tapestries and portraits, dating from 1600's and 1700's. We looked at an embroidery exhibition of very old pieces from the 1500's and 1600's. We walked through a lovely garden of flowers and herbs. That evening Amanda and I drove to the Lawrence Lacemakers' meeting of twenty-five ladies and made lace until 9 p.m. The women honored me with a gift of their carrying bag with the Lawrence Lacemakers' logo on it.

It rained the next day on our morning drive to Nottingham, and to the Lace Market Center where we watched four films about the lace machinery industry. Nottingham is where lace was first made by machines. We walked to the lace center and costume museum to see an excellent lace display. At noon we walked to the Jerusalem Pub before going to the castle, and top of the hill to look at views of the city, then we walked to the Council Hall in the center of the city, and to the summer market. We drove to Wollen Hall and did not get out of the car so did not have to go through Hoof and Mouth disease disinfectant.

One morning we drove a one hundred and twenty miles round trip to Moreton Hall above Stoke-on-Trent. It is a beautiful half-timbered house in the National Trust and dates to 1400's with large vistas of farming homes and horses and many cattle and sheep among hills and stone fences. We walked across a draw bridge and moat filled with large orange carp and entered inside the courtyard to wait for a tour of the house that was reinforced with steel in 1990 and 1993. We walked through gardens of formal cut boxwood where a gardener was still trimming them.

The next day, we drove into Nottingham and to the Sherwood Community Center to an all-day meeting of the Nottinghamshire Bobbin Lace Society. Thirty-five lacemakers came to the meeting. That evening my London lace friend phoned with driving details for my next week at her home.

The following day we drove sixty-two miles round trip to Calke Abbey, the home of a wealthy Lord Baronet until his death taxes reduced the estate. We viewed four hundred years of family history and huge gardens and a greenhouse that grew all the food for a large number of employees. I walked to the church where Sir Calke was buried when he died in 1981; he did not provide for death taxes, therefore, the estate went to the National Trust. The family saved everything over the generations, and it was interesting to see how they lived. There was a blacksmith shop, horse and carriage barns, fire wagon, and hearse on the property. That evening at Amanda's home, while watching England defeat Australia on the 4th day of their cricket match, a hedgehog came to the glass doors of the house to eat peanuts. It was an exciting first time for me to see a live hedgehog.

The next day, we left Amanda's Westwood home at 9 a.m. to drive over one hundred miles south to the London suburb Kenton home of my friend Suzanne. After lunch in the backyard in lovely August weather, we drove twenty-seven miles to Luton Museum to look at lace. Suzanne is a lace teacher and discussed the lace in the collections piece by piece with me. I learned a lot about lace from her analysis. It was the first time I had seen Bucks and Bedfordshire lace made in black thread. There were many needle lace pieces from Italy. Lace history began in the year 1560, according to the Luton Museum exhibit.

I bought the Luton Museum's *Lace Dealer's Pattern Book*, a series of pages to which snippets of lace are attached. The dealer showed the pieces, produced by the women that worked for him, and a customer picked the one wanted and requested how many yards (or pieces, if a motif). Then the dealer ordered that amount from the woman who specialized in that pattern.

After breakfast the next morning, Suzanne and I walked to the bus to Norwich Park "tube" station to get off at the Victoria and Albert Museum in South Kensington. We looked first at a fantastic USA artist, Dale Chihuly, glass exhibition. At noon we bought tea and cookies and sat in the garden eating, surrounded by more Chihuly glass displays. That afternoon we walked to the textile exhibits and viewed pieces from the 1300–1400's before going to the lace room. We spent a long time looking at all the lace pieces including Italian needle lace and Brussels lace from the 17th and 18th century, and, French and English lace from the 17th, 18th, and 19th century. We opened all twenty-eight lace drawers and pulled out one hundred frames of lace, and Suzanne explained all of them to me. There was exquisite Carrickmacross lace and some Binche lace. We finished in late afternoon and walked to the "tube" and caught a bus to Suzanne's, and she showed me her antique lace collection.

A lacemaker friend of Suzanne arrived at her home early the next morning and the three of us went by bus and "tube" to Green Park and walked to Buckingham Palace. We walked in the gardens and sat on a bench until time to get in the queue to enter the palace. We each bought a book about the palace tour before entering the first hallway. It is a pristine palace; everything in perfect condition. Beautiful ceilings and inlaid floor designs. We walked on real rugs that were soft, and many of them were red in color. There was French furniture and porcelain everywhere. I loved it! There were two throne rooms; one was also a ballroom where awards are presented. Queen Victoria's throne chair sits off to the right of the present Queen's throne. Victoria was very short so her chair is close to the floor.

We walked through the Buckingham Palace gardens and huge lawn surrounding a three and one-half acre lake. Then we walked to the Royal Mews and saw the beautiful Gold State Coach.

The next morning, Suzanne and I rode the bus and "tube" and changed trains to get off at High Street,

Kensington and walk to Kensington Palace. There were recorder phones to listen to a two hour and forty-five minute tour. We saw court costumes from the early 20th century Edward II era, and gowns of Elizabeth II, also Queen Victoria's wardrobe beginning at her age of ten years to teenage years before she was eighteen and became Queen, her Coronation robes, wedding dress, and dress she wore to Privy Council the day she became Queen, mourning dresses, and her sixty year Jubilee dress. We viewed Princess Diana's dresses, gowns, and suits.

We saw the king's staircase and apartments, the queen's apartments, Victoria's parents (the Duke and Duchess of York) rooms, and the bedroom of Victoria where she slept when she became queen. We walked to the orangery for a refreshing drink and returned to Suzanne's home to sit in the garden and work on lace pillows. Suzanne gave me two antique bobbins and two antique prickings, one was parchment.

The next day we made lace all morning. That afternoon we drove seventeen miles to the William Morris Museum. I spent an hour looking at his designs in actual fabric, wallpaper, and rugs; and learned more about his private life than I had known when studying his art at Iowa State University in my textiles and clothing major. This was the first I learned he was also famous as a poet and socialist. I learned his daughter carried on his company and made designs much like his stylized plants and flowers. I only knew about his acanthus leaf design, and that his favorite motif was a willow leaf background that he used many times.

My last day at Suzanne's home we drove sixty miles to Althorp House, located nine miles in the country, home of the Spencer family and Princess Diana's Memorial. I enjoyed seeing the art by Van Dyke and Gainsborough located all over the Althorp House. The rugs on the floors were removed and we walked on wooden floors, and along wood paneled walls. After going through the lovely palace we walked to the oval lake to see the island where Princess Diana is buried. People were there laying flowers on the grass along the memorial. The gardens and lake are larger than the gardens of Buckingham Palace.

At noon we entered the stables, a large square of buildings with an open courtyard in the center to look at the Princess Diana exhibits—her childhood years, adult years, funeral and memorial fund exhibit. Traffic returning to London was so heavy; it was a two hour drive to Suzanne's home. She showed me her lace postcards that evening.

The World Lace Organization held a world lace congress in Adelaide, the capital city of South Australia, and fifth largest city in that country. It was a thirty hour trip by plane for me to arrive in Adelaide, in the southern part of the country, via Oregon to San Francisco, to Seoul, South Korea, to Singapore, and then a nonstop flight to Adelaide.

It was my third time in Australia, having been to Melbourne both times and the capital city Canberra, before days in Sydney, and flying to Alice Springs, and a plane flight to Ayres Rock in the middle of the country. I climbed to the top of Ayres Rock, now called *Uluru,* using the chain rope support that made it possible. In Alice Springs I saw the Anzac Hill Monument to Australian and New Zealand soldiers, and the Royal Flying Doctors Service Memorial. In an Alice Springs restaurant I ordered my first camel hamburger. It was very tough! Before leaving Australia, the first two times there, we boarded a boat for a day-long excursion to the Great Barrier Reef that is two hundred miles in length and the world's largest living organism and richest marine resource.

The first time I was in Australia, I made advance reservations to fly to Fiji for several days before returning to

Oregon. I had always heard Fiji is a tropical paradise. It was an interesting experience in Fiji to take a day trip up a river to a native village where we learned about the "Kava" ceremony. Kava is the national drink made from the root of the pepper plant, and it has a slightly narcotic effect, especially to the face and lips. In the village we were escorted to a room with mats on the floor where men sat cross-legged on the floor; women sat with their legs to one side. Everyone sat in a circle. As we watched, Kava was mixed in a large carved wooden bowl. A half of a coconut shell was filled with Kava and passed to each person in the circle in turn after clapping hands once for each person. The contents of the cup were drunk in one swallow while holding the cup in both hands. Then the empty cup was returned to the host with a clap three times. Kava tasted terrible to me and I could not drink the coconut shell full of it.

Some meetings in foreign countries of the council of the world lace organization made it necessary for me to be ready to change again and again! Lacemakers call this the "hedgehog concept" of three parts: knowing what the organization is deeply passionate about; knowing what the organization can be the best in the world at; and being clear about what drives the organization's engine.

A lacemaker from Greece, on the world lace council, invited me to stay with her in an Athens suburb while attending the council meeting to plan the Greece World Lace Congress in Athens the following year. The first evening the Greek lacemaker's sister phoned from Crete and asked to speak to me and she said, "Welcome to Greece." The next day we rode a train to the stop for the Acropolis. It was an uphill walk along a garden for views and photos to the Chapel of Dimetrius before the long distance uphill walk to the Acropolis to see the restoration process. The marble stairs and walkways were slippery. We were there at the hottest time of the day and it was somewhat exhausting. This was my second visit to the Acropolis, having been there on a shore excursion from a Mediterranean cruise several years earlier, and before the start of restoration. This second time we went to see the museum behind the Parthenon and spent time there before going to a restaurant that served traditional Greek food.

One day my Greek hostess drove us through two toll roads and highways into pine-covered mountains; along many olive orchards, orange groves and tangerine groves; en route to the ancient Epidaurus Theatre, the most complete theater in Greece. It was a two hour drive. We visited the museum of artifacts and then drove another forty-five minutes to Nafplion to park by the harbor and walk the narrow, winding streets of blooming red and orange bougainvillea to the Peloponnesian Folklore Museum to see beautiful Greek costumes of the Greek islands.

Another day we rode the Athens metro and walked to the Byzantine and Christian Museum. It was explained to me that "coptic" means that Greeks occupied Egypt at the time of the first Christians. Coptic is the Greek word for Egypt. It was a few blocks walk from there to the Benaki Museum where I saw many beautiful costumes. That evening we looked at Greek lace books about lace on Crete Island.

The next year, I returned to Athens for the Greece World Lace Congress and went on a forty-minute catamaran ferry ride to an excursion on the island of Aegina. It was a bus ride through the center of the island to the temple ruins of Aphaia, followed by a drive to the city to see a lace exhibit of Rosaline lace which is my favorite lace.

My membership in the Portland Lace Society included many years of attending meetings, and I became a life member of the organization. Every two years I performed the installation of the Portland Lace Society officers; each served a two year term.

We traveled to Milford Reed's Willow Springs farm for the baptism of Anne Reed, Mark Reed's child. The Reeds worked with us in searching Palen genealogy in Greene County, New York. We went sightseeing to Mary Washington's home, mother of President George Washington; to Saint James House; to Fredericksburg Spotsylvania National Military Park; to Kenmore, George Washington's sister's home; to James Monroe's Law Office; to Rising Sun Tavern of George Washington's youngest brother; and to Woodrow Wilson's Museum and birth home at Stanton.

When the Milford Reeds and my husband and I were retired we were invited to be their guests at their time-share on the Outer Banks at Kill Devil Hills, North Carolina. They drove us to many historic sites of that state including another visit to Williamsburg, and to Appomattox Court House National Park to the house next to the courthouse where General Lee surrendered to General Grant to end the Civil War on Palm Sunday in 1865.

In twelve days at the Reed suite in Kill Devil Hills, North Carolina, we drove all of the Outer Banks, and to all the lighthouses along the Outer Banks. We toured the Palace of Tryon of the first Governor of the Colony. Another day we drove to the Wright Bros. Memorial National Park to view exhibits and a program about the Wright's airplane. We drove to Roanoke Island and Elizabethan Gardens and to Fort Raleigh that included a film about the Lost Colony, and a walk to the fort excavations. We rode a ferry across to Ocracoke Island to see that lighthouse and stopped at Cape Hatteras and Brodie lighthouses.

Another day we visited Murfreesboro historic houses, the college, and old stores, and William Rea Museum to see the Gatling Gun and Indian artifacts, and visited the John Wheeler House. We drove to Virginia Beach area and to Surrey. A Northeaster blew in one night and the Atlantic Ocean was rough with high waves that we watched from the veranda of the Reed's Kill Devil Hills suite.

We drove to Roanoke Island to the state aquarium and bought whelk shells. Historic Edenton, North Carolina, (population 5,000) was our next destination. We visited the James Iredell House, 1773–1816, Cowan County Courthouse 1767, and Cupola House 1725. Then we drove to Windsor, North Carolina, to see the Hope Plantation home of Governor Stone and the King Bazemore 1763 Plantation House. Next, we enjoyed Jamestown exhibits and a movie at Jamestown National Park about the Jamestown Colony. We walked to the Pocahontas statue and to the John Smith statue. All this early history of our country brought the realization of how much change there has been in our country.

Both of us were retired when we went to Nairobi, Kenya, and we celebrated our 40th wedding anniversary at the conclusion of a wildlife safari that included a hot-air balloon ride over wildlife in the savannah. Our anniversary dinner was at Africa's greatest eating experience, Carnivore Restaurant, located not far from Jomo Kenyatta International Airport. It has an African meat specialty menu: Masai cow, eland, ostrich, zebra, crocodile, camel, and venison, served alongside lamb, pork and ribs, beef, and chicken, roasted on traditional Masai swords over charcoal. We served our eight guests traveling with us three bottles of French champagne, and everyone gave toasts to us. A tour member sang a solo, our favorite song, "I Left My Heart in San Francisco," and we were presented a congratulatory card signed by everyone—a unique anniversary celebration in a unique place in the world.

Margaret Krug Palen

CHAPTER 12
The Holy Land and Egypt

In retirement my lifelong dream of going to Jerusalem and the Holy Land came true seven different times. Each visit to the Holy Land started with an evening of relaxation in an Israel city along the Mediterranean coastline to rest from the many hours of an Israel El Al Airline transatlantic flight that began with a cross continental flight across USA. In the seven times I was in Israel I learned that it is a nation of many people living together with the time honored realization they are God's chosen people.

In my youth I sang the beautiful "Jerusalem song" in Christmas programs, and I dreamed that one day I would see the city. My studies in geography and history did not give me an insight to the Bible Lands as did going there. I remembered learning Isaiah 66:10 "Rejoice with Jerusalem, and be glad for her, all you who love her." To see, to hear, to feel, to touch the land of the prophets, the place where Jesus was born, lived, taught, suffered, died, and rose triumphantly became real in my life while being there seven different times.

I saw where Abraham prepared to offer Isaac on Mount Moriah, where Solomon built the first temple, now the site of the Dome of the Rock and a Muslim mosque, where Jesus prayed in Gethsemane and the Garden Tomb. I traveled the Jericho Road, sailed on the Sea of Galilee, and stood by the Pool of Bethesda; each an inspiring experience.

At Mt. Carmel I saw the historic location of the confrontation between Elijah and the four hundred prophets of Baal during the reign of Ahab and Jezebel. A statue commemorates that historic event.

Each time in Israel I saw where the Dead Sea scrolls were discovered, and went to Masada where the Romans ended the Israelite nation in 73 A.D. A walk inside Masada's large water cavern was interesting. We traveled to the Dead Sea and went in the salty water. It is only possible to float! Several times we stayed at a hotel by the Dead Sea.

Jerusalem has been a tourist center for over twenty-one centuries. Many years ago the people who visited Jerusalem were known as pilgrims, and there was a time before Herod when pilgrims were provided full accommodations free of charge because it was said that Jerusalem belonged to all the people of Israel.

As recently as eighty years ago, the journey to Jerusalem was still a difficult, hazardous undertaking. The ascent from Jaffa was made on horseback, by wagon or even on foot and could take two or three days, and many people were attacked by bandits or wild animals. I read the writings of Mark Twain and Herman Melville that are particularly explicit about Jerusalem when the country in general was quite desolate and poverty stricken.

I traveled Israel in the age of computerized hotel bookings and electronic site guides, and a visit to the Holy City was controlled and comfortable. Psalm 122 came back to my memory in Jerusalem: "I was glad when they said unto me, Let us go into the house of the Lord. Our feet shall stand within thy gates, O Jerusalem....Pray for the peace of Jerusalem: they shall prosper that love thee."

My husband and I were in Israel on our 35th wedding anniversary and we went to Cana's "wedding church" where Jesus performed the miracle at a wedding of turning water into wine. A minister in our tour group performed a remarriage ceremony for us. After the ceremony we walked across the street to a reception center and celebrated the occasion.

It was a great blessing to be a pilgrim in the Holy Land seven times over the span of thirteen years. A highlight each time was a visit to the church of the Holy Sepulcher. I walked by crowded markets, shops, and past souvenir stores to the greatest church in the world virtually continuously venerated since the time of Roman Emperor Constantine the Great. It is the only church in the world where six of the most ancient Christian denominations worship side by side. The Greek Orthodox, Roman Catholic, and Armenian Orthodox churches are known as major communities with rights of possession and usage at the holy place. The Coptic, Ethiopian, and Syrian Orthodox churches are deemed minor communities, with rights of usage, but not rights of possession at the holy places. St. John of Damascus, writing in the eighth century, called the Church of the Holy Sepulcher, also known as the Anastasis or Church of the Resurrection, the "mother of all the churches."

The Church of the Holy Sepulcher is the only church where first century Herodian, second century Hadrianic, fourth century Constantinian, eleventh century Byzantine, twelfth century Crusader, nineteenth century neo-Byzantine, and twentieth century modern masonry are visible in one place.

Jesus was executed outside Jerusalem in 30 or 33 A.D. Ten years later, the places of the crucifixion and burial were incorporated within the walls of the expansion of the city. Decades later, these places were buried beneath immense dumps of rubble brought in by the Romans to level the area. Golgotha, the place of crucifixion, was still pointed out inside the city three centuries later. It served as a landmark for excavations which discovered several rock-cut tombs under the rubble. One of the tombs was immediately hailed as the tomb of Christ.

The Gospels imply that the crucifixion and burial of Jesus took place outside the city walls. When Bishop Makarios of Jerusalem sought the burial place ca. 325, he excavated a site within the walled city and located a tomb that he and others accepted as the burial place of Christ, and it has ever since been the focal point of the Church of the Holy Sepulcher in its successive forms. The Emperor Constantine ordered Golgotha and the tomb be preserved and embellished and a great church be erected beside them. During the Constantine period and later, the tomb appears in a wide range of media, paintings on wood and vellum, ivory carving, stone sculpture, mosaic, metal, pottery, and glass.

In 1808, the Church of the Holy Sepulcher was extensively damaged by fire. An earthquake in 1927 threatened the whole structure with collapse, but it was not until March 1947 that it was strapped together by a cradle of steel girders put in position by the government of Palestine, the last of their work in the Church of the Holy Sepulcher. Inside the tomb the actual burial couch is usually covered with embroidered cloths, and the ledges around the couch are adorned with many candles.

We were in Jerusalem on its 3000th year and signed the memorial book and any of our descendants who go there can ask to find our signature to confirm that we were there in that celebration year. We went to Jerusalem's Hadassah Forest and planted a sapling tree with our own hands in memory of our first child, Nancy Ann Palen; that will beautify the ancient vistas of the Land of the Bible. It was a giving of something of ourselves, and while the tree grows it will improve the quality of Israel's environment. We returned three years later for our 42nd wedding anniversary, our sixth time in the Holy Land, and went to south Jerusalem's Hadassah Forest to look at the tree we planted in memory of our loved one, and observed it was growing and bushing out.

It was amazing to see excavations at Megiddo, and to overlook the Jezreel Valley, the site of Biblical warfare; all reveal a 7,000 year old history and the layered presence of twenty cities.

Each of my seven times in Israel we rode a boat on the Sea of Galilee, and went to Tiberias, Capernaum, Mount of Beatitudes, ancient Tabgha, Nazareth, and places familiar in the Bible. One year we were there in February and it snowed on us in Nazareth.

The holy city of Jerusalem was an important destination for me. I envisioned in my youth a picture of Jerusalem that always stayed with me: Revelation 21: "Then I saw a new heaven and a new earth....And I saw the holy city, the new Jerusalem, coming down out of heaven from God." Jerusalem became real to me each time I was there. At a young age I was assigned to memorize Psalm 122: "I was glad when they said to me, 'Let us go to the house of the Lord. Now our feet are standing within your gates, O Jerusalem."

The Western Wall in Jerusalem dominated my attention with its huge building blocks still in place that are left over from the destruction of the Second Temple by Roman forces in 70 A.D. I prayed at the Western Wall, and placed prayer requests to return to Jerusalem on paper that I rolled up and inserted in the cracks and crevasses of the wall. That prayer came true seven times over a period of thirteen years.

We viewed the Holocaust Museum and also the Children's Museum; both sad to observe that six million Jews were killed during the Holocaust.

Jerusalem's Dome of the Rock was important to me. We paid admission to go inside it and observed the large rock where it is thought Abraham planned, as directed, to slay his son until God stopped him.

The St. Stephen's Gate of the Old City, marked by Crusader lions carved in the stone wall, was also special to me. St. Stephen was the name of the congregation where I was baptized and confirmed, and I learned about that saint at an early age.

Each time we were in Israel we went to the Shrine of the Book to see the Dead Sea Scrolls history. Also, each time we took communion in the Garden Tomb.

Both Bethlehem and Jerusalem are built high on hills. The seventh time we were in Bethlehem it was under the control of the Palestinians and had a wall built around it that separated it from Jerusalem. Each time we visited the Church of the Holy Sepulcher to see the historic place where Jesus was born. The Church of the Nativity, as it is frequently called, was not the stable I remembered from Sunday school and bible study pictures, but I was moved by the layers of construction and ornamentation that have existed around that holy site for nearly 2000 years. Each time we were there we visited a Bethlehem souvenir shop, and the following Christmas they remembered us by sending holiday greetings to Oregon from Bethlehem.

We went to Egypt six of the seven times we were in Israel. Several times we drove across the Israel border and crossed the Sinai Peninsula into Africa via a Suez Canal ferry. Other times we flew from Israel to Cairo, the largest city in Africa. Each time we spent hours in Cairo's Egyptian Museum to see the mummies of Pharaoh Ramses II and others, and many artifacts from the tomb of Pharaoh Tutankhamen. It brought back my memory of studying Egyptian historic textiles in my major field for my bachelor's degree. In Coptic Cairo we always went to the Coptic Hanging Church, and to see the crypt where the Holy Family stayed that is now St. Barbara Church.

Each time in Cairo we went to the pyramids of Giza and the Sphinx, and always rode a camel. It was exciting to ride a camel at the Giza Pyramids. I climbed up to the great pyramid entrance and went inside, with the assistance of a guide, to see the inner room burial vault.

In Egypt we flew from Cairo to Luxor and to Aswan on the eastern bank of the Nile River. We crossed the edge of the Sahara to Abu Simbel and visited the great temples and sixty-five foot statues of Ramses II before we boarded a Nile cruise ship. The Nile cruise is the greatest cruise in the world. Included on the cruise ship is a guide on board that takes passengers to the temple stops along the way.

Cruise food is so abundant and beautifully presented it is easy to choose only the hot food, and only look at the beautifully displayed salads. In third world countries, such as Egypt, it was important not to eat salads or any food that has not been exposed to heat. The common bacteria, even on equipment of those that prepared the food, could upset the physical system. It was important to remember that we are immune to only the common bacteria on the continent we were born on. We were careful about food selection each time we were in Egypt, and never experienced illness.

We cruised the Nile River after going to Aswan to see the big dam and the ruins of one of the temples where Christians lived to avoid the Romans. The first time our cruise ship was Presidential Nile Cruises *Nile Symphony*, and when we returned the next year our cruise ship was MS *Nile Marquis*. In the next years we cruised the Nile River on Inter Egypt's *The Serenade* and at the turn of the century we were on MS *Jasmin*.

Nile cruise ships stop at Kom Ombo Temple with a guided tour of the historic place. We stopped at Edfu for a horse drawn carriage ride to the Temple of Horus, Egypt's best preserved temple. We went inside to the Perfume Room and saw hieroglyphics of one-hundred-eighty recipes for making perfume on the walls. The origin of perfume is Egypt, and not the French excavators that discovered the room, researched it, and made claim to France being the first to make perfumes.

The cruise ships stop at the temple to Isis on Philae Island. One cruise we went fifty miles north from Luxor to the Dendera ruins, Ptolemaic-era Temple of Hathor and Qena, where we saw inscriptions from when Queen Cleopatra and Mark Anthony were there. Every tour we visited Luxor Temple and Karnak Temple, both fascinating. One visit we attended an evening program at Luxor Temple to listen to a dramatic presentation of its history.

In Luxor there is a link with the great discoveries in the Valley of the Kings. We rode horse-drawn carriages in the city, and sailed on a ferry from there to the Valley of the Kings where New Kingdom Pharaohs were buried in elaborate tombs. At the Valley of the Kings and Valley of the Queens we saw many inscriptions and writings on limestone walls, also etchings of owls, birds, fish and King Ramsey I and Ramsey VIII.

England's Lord Carnarvon financed the excavations in Egypt's Valley of the Kings and was a lover of art, and also a highly skilled archaeologist. His friend was Howard Carter the Egyptologist. Axel Munthe was known to both and was fascinated with the artistry of the old Egyptians and witnessed the final unsealing of the innermost coffin, and the uncovering, after more than 3,000 years, of the dead Pharaoh. We were excited to enter King Tuts tomb on one of our visits in the Valley of the Kings. Each year we were in

Egypt we toured the Valley of the Kings, the Valley of Queens, and Al-Deir-Al Bahari Temple.

The Millennium was an important time for many people to go to The Holy Land. My travel agent suggested we go the last of November and first of December 1999 to avoid the rush at the change of the century. We wanted to go to both Israel and to Egypt on a Nile cruise, and we were thankful we did go early because there was of an outbreak of hostility in Israel December 31–January 1, at the change of the centuries, that made it impossible for tourists to go there. The last time we were in Israel was in the first decade of the twenty-first century. In the years after that conditions continued to be unfavorable in that part of the world.

Margaret Krug Palen

CHAPTER 13
American Making a Difference

In foreign countries I learned that it is impossible to actually experience another culture as a tourist, and I definitely discovered this in my first foreign assignment with the International Executive Services Corps. The organization headquarters are in Washington, D.C., and I went abroad for two months to work on their project in Ghana, West Africa.

According to the present state of knowledge, it is highly probable that Africa is the cradle of humanity. When I lived among the citizens of a country in Africa I began to understand their lives and world view. Culture can be defined as the total way of life of a particular people. It includes how they obtain their food, what they eat and drink, how they dress, how they organize their community life and marriage, their language and how they practice their religion, and what music they play. This I experienced each time I worked on foreign assignments in six different countries.

Ghana is too near the equator to have four seasons a year. The only changes during the year are the rainy and dry seasons. I could see the Sahara Desert and the sand dunes below the airplane on my flight across Africa to Accra, Ghana. My seat was in the upstairs first class section of only eight passengers.

My husband was sent to accompany me on the Ghana project because I would be the only white person living in an African native village. He sent his forestry career qualifications in to the organization and inquired if he could meet with someone in the Ghana Forestry Department. He was given the name of the Regional Forestry Office Project Leader and the location of the Ghana Regional Education Office.

We lived in Accra, the capital city of Ghana, in the Shangri-La Hotel, enabling us in free moments to see the city's museums and national monuments. We were given a million cedis in Ghana money for our expenses, the first time we had ever had a million of any kind of money.

The first day in Accra, we met the USA ambassador and his wife. He presided at a USA flag raising ceremony and gave a speech in honor of the 4th of July even though it was the 29th of June. Ghana has a national independence holiday on July 4, therefore, the early USA celebration. At a picnic that followed, my husband was hungry and ate salad thinking it was safe to eat it at a celebration of USA citizens. That night he became ill with vomiting and diarrhea. I did not eat anything that did not have heat applied to it according to my medical instructions. I gave my husband Imodium tablets that I carried in my emergency medical kit, and he rapidly recovered.

The client for my project was Dr. Esther Ocloo, five foot tall and eighty years old. Her residence was in Accra and she came to our hotel to meet us. She explained the project I was to work on with her was to make a difference in the lives of young, unmarried Ghanian women so they could support themselves.

The next day, we were transported through many villages to the Volta Hotel for lunch, and a drive to Akosombo Dam and to Peki Blengo village. There are ten Peki villages and we drove to the one that had the African Women's Entrepreneurial Training Center. My client, who preferred I call her "Auntie Esther," was there to meet us and gave us a tour of the campus that was built by Germany many years ago. She attended the school when she was young, and when she became a recipient of a $10,000 award for women's projects in the world she bought the vacant school and was in the process of converting it into a training center for unmarried Ghanian women.

Monday morning I was formally introduced to twenty young women, and I watched a teacher working with them to make biscuits to be packaged and sold in the village. That afternoon "Auntie Esther" and her driver took us to her school board members' homes to introduce me and my husband to them. We discussed concerns about learning clothing construction, and I learned one of the board members taught tie-dye to the students at "Auntie Esther's" school.

The next day there was rain and lightning; thunderstorms all morning. In the afternoon I walked to the Peki Hospital with one of the kitchen students to observe a class being held for them about bathing a baby, and a bed-making "military style" demonstration. Two of the students walked back with me, and we stopped at the Peki Vocational Institute where twenty-five girls were studying dressmaking.

I observed "Auntie Esther" teaching students first aid, health and family planning classes. Only one of the students could speak English, and one day she took me to visit a dressmaker's shop in the village.

Ken helped me measure the large room in the AWETC campus building that was my challenge to convert for the teaching of clothing construction. It was my job to draw a floor plan for the use of sewing machines and tables for the construction of clothing in the room.

I prepared all the food for the two of us each day in the building we lived in which was separate from the school kitchen. Before leaving Accra for the village of Peki Blengo we were taken grocery shopping and told to purchase a large supply of food because we were instructed not to eat with the students.

The first native food that was eaten daily we learned about was fufu, a staple paste made from ground cassava that is eaten with ground-nut stew and sauce. The method of the natives with fufu is to swallow, not chew it. We did not taste or eat fufu because it is processed without heat and not compatible with our health.

The first weekend the students on the AWETC campus used all the water so we did not have water in our building for any use. "Auntie Esther's" driver drove us to Okosombo's Volta Hotel where we stayed over the weekend and enjoyed the luxury of hot water for baths, and I washed out our laundry and hung it on our hotel room veranda. We had both TV and radio, a luxury as there was none at the school campus in Peki Blengo. The hotel food was also a luxury for us that we relished.

That Sunday we went on a cruise on the *Dodie Princess* that stopped two hours at Dodie Island where we ate a barbecued chicken lunch. Later, on the return to Peki Blengo we stopped for diesel and had more time for additional grocery shopping. We also stopped to buy a "talking drum" that fascinated us from a roadside vendor demonstrating it just outside the village of Peki.

We bought two drums from roadside vendors while in Ghana. Their drums are the oldest and best known in traditional Ghana music activities. They are used for social, military, and political occasions for talking, singing, and dancing, and are carved from the Kyendur tree, and most are covered with black antelope skin. The atumpan drum (talking drum), which is covered in elephant skin, is used to transmit messages. In festivals it "speaks" of trait and achievements. A few days after we bought the first drum the students on our campus borrowed it from us to accompany their singing several evenings, and in days later returned it to us. The drums we bought in Ghana have resided many years in the living room of our USA home.

My second week the Unity Dressmakers Group came to the campus to meet with "Auntie Esther" and me. We did a "show and tell" about a future sewing course, and I discussed changes in clothing construction they would learn. Everything that week was preparation for the official opening of the school along with the graduation of the first class of students. An exhibition of food products made by the students was set up in time for the event. The students borrowed a shirt from my husband to launder and exhibit it to show their knowledge of how to care for men's clothing.

The first group to arrive the evening before the campus ceremonies was the World Sustainable End of Hunger Foundation (SEHUF) from Europe and USA. "Auntie Esther" brought them to meet me and we walked to the exhibition. The campus center was transformed during the day to be ready for graduation the next day, and the students were all in their best dresses and each of them had a fancy hairdo. They began selling their food products immediately to the visitors.

It was 11 a.m. the next day before all the dignitaries arrived for the official opening of AWETC followed by graduation exercises for the twenty young women who completed the first courses in food preparation, food preservation, and home management. Following the ribbon cutting ceremony at the gate of the campus, donations to the campus were given in a fund drive for the future of the school. My husband and I donated 150,000 cedis of the money paid to us upon arrival to use for our expenses. The tribal chief was in attendance and he donated 100,000 cedis. Speeches and music followed with a specially prepared buffet lunch for everyone. It was the only time my husband and I ate in the student's dining hall. There was a large selection of food prepared, and we carefully chose to eat only cooked chicken and two kinds of rice, yams and steamed corn flour rolls. Fortunately, it was all hot and completely cooked through, and we did not become ill from eating with students.

At 5 p.m. a torrential downpour began and lasted until 7 p.m. At 8 p.m. one of the students knocked on our door and brought a cookbook to give me the recipe for cocoyam beef stew that I saw her making in the kitchen a day earlier.

The next day, "Auntie Esther" knocked on our door and was ready to get the students together for a final goodbye as it was time for them to leave the campus. She requested I give a speech and the closing remarks after which she, as center director, along with teacher Grace formed a receiving line with me at the door to say "goodbye" with handshakes. The graduated students boarded a bus and it took another half hour for the men to load all their luggage on top of the bus and cover it, to protect it from rain, before they were ready to depart from the campus.

The weeks that followed had conferences about my plan of work. "Auntie Esther" wanted to know more about the degree of improvement and level of dressmaker's skills, which necessitated my visit to many dressmakers in the area to observe the skills that needed improvement. She also took me to a textile weaving room where there were new weaving students for a one year study at the school.

"Auntie Esther" discussed with me her plans for the future of AWETC. She planned to fence in a flock of two hundred chickens, plant a vegetable garden, grow mushrooms, and raise snails to make it possible to become a self-supporting school. She discussed the cost per student and the income taken in on the last course, and the official opening ceremony donations.

Ghana, West Africa, conference with "Auntie Esther."

There were more rain storms that awakened us in the next nights. We were definitely there at the rainy season of the year.

"Auntie Esther" made arrangements for my husband and me to accompany her on a visit to eight dressmaker shops in Peki Blengo and Peki Avetile that included a men's tailor shop. I noted prices, kinds of garments being made, sewing machine models used and whether electric or hand power, cost of garments, problems in construction, and the number of apprentices. Hems and seams were in need of standardization. I needed this observation in order to help "Auntie Esther and her teachers make a difference in teaching students. It poured rain on us as we toured, making it necessary to delay our return to the car by a half hour at one shop.

We were given another weekend in Accra and we learned more about the Gold Coast when it was a British Colony. Ghana originally drew the attention of Europeans in the 16th and 17th centuries for its storehouses of gold and ivory. In time they found slaves more lucrative and built dozens of stone forts, that still stand, to protect their human cargoes. A driver drove us to Cape Coast and Elmina and coastal fishing towns about sixty and seventy-five miles west of Accra. We viewed slave castles, now UNESCO historic sites, where slaves were exported to the Americas.

We would never forget Kakum National Park, a first experience for us to go on a canopy walkway above the tree line. It is the only one on the African continent. A 350 meter long bridge connects seven treetops and is constructed of wire rope, aluminum ladders, wooden planks and safety netting. In order to protect the trees, no nails or bolts pierce the tree bark. It was a little scary to walk on the moving walkway that high above the ground. The park is a unique rain forest located only thirty-three kilometers north of Cape Coast.

It was my fourth week in Ghana when one of "Auntie Esther's" teachers made arrangements for a driver, and she went with my husband and me to the Ho Volta Region Museum for a tribal visit. We then drove to Agotime Kpetoe, near the Togo border, to see the Kente weavers. We visited the village birthplace of Kente cloth, especially of interest to me because I learned about it while studying for my textile degree at Iowa State. It was an exciting experience to see weavers sitting outside over a large part of the village, and close to the streets, making it possible for us to view them by just driving along the streets. We stopped so I could look closer at the weaving and my husband took photos. I bought three Kente cloth pieces at a store for illustration in working with "Auntie Esther" and village dressmakers.

We returned to Ho to find the Regional Forester in his office. My husband had an interesting half hour conference with him. When we arrived back at the campus, two Peki Blengo dressmakers were there to meet us and give us two matching Ghana's national costumes of Kente cloth they had made to fit us.

Conferences were held with "Auntie Esther" and the Ghana International Executive Corps Director and Deputy Director about my project that was to provide information for writing a grant. I was still working on the assessment and needed more time. Later, I went to watch "Auntie Esther" and several kitchen workers who were experimenting with recipes and a cost/profit analysis for future sales.

One weekend with "Auntie Esther," on the way to Accra, we stopped at Akosombo Textile Company so I could view wax prints, super prints and funeral prints. It was interesting to see the designs and consider them for use at her school. I discussed them with "Auntie Esther" to determine her interest in them for her school clothing construction classes.

I could not sleep at the Shangri-La Hotel because I missed the noise outside our window on the campus where a local mother daily pounded fufu under a tree right outside our window.

The next week, my client "Auntie Esther" picked me up at the hotel to drive to Makola Market to view fabrics and sewing machines. I saw sixteen different sewing machines from Germany, and industrial machines—Singers from Great Britain. A lively discussion resulted with "Auntie Esther" about which sewing machines to purchase for her school. Then we drove to Madina to see a sewing and silk screen factory. I learned my client "Auntie Esther" hoped I would look for garment market possibilities in USA, and that I would assess the type of clothing production that qualified for export. She was determining the cost to open a market in Ghana. That week I spent time on report work—writing, changing and editing the assessment objectives and accomplishments.

The following week "Auntie Esther" and her driver took me to Katenit Textile Factory in the industrial part of the Accra where we met in an air-conditioned office for an hour with her daughter, discussing the exporting of garments to USA, and the problems involved. We looked in on some of the sewers working on Singer and Pfaff industrial machines. We drove to Madina and visited Providence Dressmaking Home where sixty-five girls, some as young as fifteen to sixteen years, studied sewing for two to three years. This helped to keep girls who were out of school off the streets. The President of Madina Dressmakers Association served us lunch before taking us to five tailor and dressmaking shops to observe sewing machines and the skills of the workers. It gave me a more accurate idea of what was available locally.

The remainder of my time in the month of August required renting a typewriter at the business center and typing a progress report, making photo copies, and writing a final report. It took time to finish the floor plan for the campus clothing building, and to make a final copy. I organized and typed a teachers' clothing construction course manual for "Auntie Esther" to use with her next class of students in the clothing construction building.

My husband typed a two-page forestry critique for the Ghana Forestry Department. A forester came to Accra one evening to play tennis with a friend, and asked to meet with my husband. When my husband turned in his critique he was given a book, *Field Guide to the Forest Trees of Ghana*.

We visited Ghana's National Museum's "Man's Endless Struggle" and saw contemporary Ghanaian art by Dr. Ampofo that stands in front of the Museum of Accra that was opened in 1957 by the Duchess of Kent. We were reminded of the saying by Aggrey of Africa (an intellectual, missionary and teacher, and a native of the Gold Coast (modern Ghana) who immigrated to USA): "If you educate a man, you educate an individual, if you educate a woman, you educate a family."

We looked at displays of beads, fertility dolls, stools, chief's regalia, an Egyptian exhibit, and items from several other African nations, and artifacts from excavations of the Stone Age and Iron Age.

I was given a date for debriefing by US AID. A day earlier I had a meeting with my client Dr. Esther Ocloo ("Auntie Esther"), the Ghana director of education, and the project manager to discuss my final report. My client seemed pleased with my report. We all signed the report.

My debriefing by US AID was at the U.S. Embassy where we went through security to the deputy ambassador's office as the ambassador was out of town. I was given a certificate award, an expression of appreciation for my service. A farewell dinner that evening was attended by all the volunteers in Ghana at that time.

International work gave me a view of world policy, and I learned how my own country is viewed by people of other cultures.

ACDI/VOCA is a private nonprofit organization established to promote broad-based economic growth and development of civil society in emerging democracies and developing countries. Volunteers in Overseas Cooperative Assistance operates with Agricultural Cooperative

Development International. I accepted African projects: thirty-four days in Ethiopia, and a month in Mozambique, that was Africa's poorest country at that time.

My job assignment as a consultant was to help a designated person carry out their assigned task and to make a difference in what was accomplished. The person assigned to me was called the consultant's "counterpart." I was not an official of the government, and had no authority to require action. It was challenging, and I discovered it was possible to make a difference in accomplishments in the countries where I worked.

Ethiopia and Eritrea were in a two-year Horn of Africa border war that caused the lowering of airplane window shades prior to my landing at Addis Ababa Airport. Ethiopia is near the equator in East Africa and is about the size of Texas and California combined. The capital Addis Ababa is 7,800 feet in altitude with a population of four to five million. The majority of the Ethiopian population is poor and dependent on rain-fed agriculture that grows on poor soil. My work there was based on my years of Agricultural Extension Service work with 4-H Clubs in America.

I had time to make Bucks Point "Little Hearts" lace on my travel pillow on the tray on the plane chair back in front of me while flying from Detroit in a wind which shortened the time to six hours and eighteen minutes to Amsterdam. I saw beautiful views of the German and Austrian Alps covered in snow while flying to Rome. Both the Amsterdam and Rome airports were decorated for Christmas though it was already January 7th and in those countries it was the Epiphany season.

After checking in the Rome Hilton Hotel I rode the hotel shuttle to the train station in downtown Rome where I boarded a bus to Vatican City. It was January and still the

A Different World

Christmas season before Epiphany. I had been to the Vatican in earlier years, and this time it was exciting to see a large crèche by the Egyptian obelisk in the center of Vatican square that had a tall Christmas tree standing beside it all decorated with straw ornaments and lights.

It was the Holy Jubilee Year 2000. I waited in line twenty minutes to enter St. Peter's Basilica through the large thirteen foot high bronze door that is only opened and closed about every twenty-five years. I was one of about twenty-five million people that made the Jubilee pilgrimage through the Holy Door of St. Peter's Basilica at the beginning of the twenty-first century. Inside the Basilica I was overwhelmed at the loveliness of the architecture, and the most beautiful crèche I have ever seen. A candlelight service was in progress at the altar. It was the first time I could take as much time as I wanted to wander and look at the architecture and decoration. In earlier years, when I was there, I was on a tour and had to follow a guide that did not pause very long going through the building.

Returning to the Hilton Hotel I went to the lobby restaurant for dinner, and met my co-worker when he came to my table to meet me. His flights from USA were late and he was tired. We met again the next morning at the Alitalia Airlines departure gate to fly to Milan. There were beautiful views of Italian Alps covered in snow on a four and one-half hour flight to Jiddah, Saudi Arabia. Many Arab families with children were on board. We had another three and one-half hour flight to Addis Ababa, Ethiopia, and a rough landing at midnight.

It was 1:30 a.m. when we checked in the Hilton Hotel that had a beautiful, tall, lighted Christmas tree in the lobby. The hotel had a plaque: "November 3, 1969 in the 40th year of his reign his Imperial Majesty Haile Selassie I, Emperor of Ethiopia inaugurated this hotel."

I recalled the Bible quotation: "Can the Ethiopian change his skin or the leopard his spots? Then may ye also do good..."

I was awake early the next morning for buffet breakfast and a walk in the hotel gardens around the swimming pool. Roses and Poinsettias were in full bloom and there were many beautiful succulents. A mini-golf and tennis courts, putting green, and squash field were all inside the walls surrounding the hotel. The large Jacaranda trees with lovely purple blossoms were the first thing I noticed in the city.

I walked through the hotel gate, and a friendly Orthodox English Ethiopian told me about the short distance to the palace. I walked there and stood in front of the flag-covered casket of Emperor Haile Selassie. His picture was on top of the casket. He had been dead since 27 August 1975 (at age 83) following a coup d'état. He reigned 1930–1974. Emperor Haile Selassie was the 226th descendant of Solomon and the Queen of Sheba. A palace guide told me the history of King Solomon and the Queen of Sheba, then opened a door in the floor for me to walk to a lower level and he showed me the tombs of former kings. Later that same year, after I returned home, I heard on the TV news that Emperor Haile Selassie's casket had just been entombed on the 15th of November 2000 in Holy Trinity Cathedral, Addis Ababa.

In elementary school Bible history, I learned King Solomon and the Queen of Sheba had a son. When the Queen of Sheba returned home she gave birth in Ethiopia to King Solomon's son and named him Menelek. In Ethiopia I learned she came from Tigre in Northern Ethiopia where it was considered natural that a woman should hold supreme power. Today there are thousands of "descendants of Menelek" who have observed the Old Testament and Jewish customs since childhood, and live in Gondar, Ethiopia. The teachings and traditions have been passed down from generation to generation for almost 3,000 years!

My co-worker and I met after breakfast the first morning, and a driver came to take us to meet our project program officer. We were briefed by the Ethiopian Country Director.

We then went to the USA Embassy to register, fill out forms, and show passports. We drove to Oromia Co-op office, the second organization requesting our project. We only had time to meet the deputy coordinator as the director was in the hospital. We drove to USAID office for an appointment about the "gender issue" for my project. We drove to a store to buy bottled water before returning to the hotel for lunch. That afternoon we exchanged money at the bank, and had an appointment with the director of extension at the agriculture department before we returned to Oromia Co-op office for a meeting with the program officer.

Every day was busy with appointments at the Ministry of Agriculture office to meet our extension service counterpart. He had written "Guide Line For Involving Rural Youth In Rural Development Programs." Communism took over Ethiopia and abandoned the youth programs that Emperor Haile Selassie organized that were similar to USA 4-H Clubwork. It was my co-worker's and my challenge to plan the reestablishment of the 4-H Club youth program that would make a difference for Ethiopia's youth.

I quickly learned Ethiopia is a very religious country. There were Christian icons on computer desktops in every office. I was immediately introduced to the nickel metal crosses that priests use to greet parishioners. They do not shake hands, instead they touch the top of a cross to the forehead of the person they are greeting, and then tip the bottom end of the cross to the person's lips where it is kissed.

My schedule was so busy that for leisure I sometimes worked bobbin lace on my travel pillow before time to go to the lobby or to drive to Dibandiba Co-op or Lumee Oromia Union Co-ops. On the way we saw teff harvest in process and stopped to visit with farmers. Teff is cut with a sickle and looks like miniature wheat. The straw is a beautiful gold color. Farmers were separating teff grain from the straw when we were there by throwing forkfuls of it in the air and letting the wind separate the grain from the straw. White teff is the most expensive and is a gluten-free grain. We also saw red teff, thought to be more nutritious.

A drive to the Southern Region of Ethiopia began at 8 a.m. with a stop at the Addis Ababa office for a conference with the administrative officer before driving seven hours, including a stop for lunch at the Langano Hotel on a lake, then over a rough road to Awassa. I saw two storks in a creek bed and an ostrich farm along the way. There were many horse-drawn carts and donkeys carrying loads, and many cattle were always with a herder.

We drove in the Rift Valley all day. I saw tall termite mounds for the first time and lots of acacia trees, and cactus of several kinds, and there were weaver birds in the trees. Millions of people were threatened with famine in southern Ethiopia because the government spent its meager resources on the Eritrean–Ethiopian War. We checked into Awassa's Pinna Hotel that had placed a small lighted Christmas tree in my room in observance of the Epiphany season.

We drove to the co-op office to meet the head officer of the Southern Regional State Co-op. He welcomed us with cups of hot tea as it was 3 p.m. when we arrived. We toured the coffee co-op drying racks where sixty people were hand sorting washed coffee beans, and we walked to the metal storehouse where coffee beans were sacked in 120-pound bags. We introduced our project idea to the workers, and found out they had never thought about it.

Ethiopia project.

The next day, we checked out of the Pinna Hotel and traveled early in the cool of the morning. We saw monkeys, a large herd of camels, and oxen plowing by pulling a walking plow. When we finally arrived in Addis Ababa, diplomats filled the lobby of the hotel for a wedding. Often at this time of year, there were large wedding receptions in the hotel.

My co-worker and I rode a hotel shuttle to the airport to fly on Ethiopian Airlines to Bahir Dar in the north of the country. Ethiopia and Eritrea were involved in a two-year Horn of Africa border war causing the closing of airplane window shades before landing at an airport in the north of Ethiopia. We were flying over a military zone of Ethiopia's war with Eritrea in the north of the country.

We checked into a hotel that was only four years old, but had mosquitoes in the rooms. My co-worker walked with me to the closest store and we bought mosquito spray, and immediately sprayed our hotel rooms. A big siren went off whenever it was time for the Muslims call to prayer.

We drove to a cereal co-op that was forty kilometers of rough road to meet an hour with their board of directors. I could not understand the interpreter, and did not get anything out of the meeting.

In Bahir Dar we met with the deputy head of the Ministry of Agriculture and learned there were 4,000 extension staff in the region. That evening, a Focus Group of four young men came to our hotel and met with us. We discussed organization of a youth group. My co-worker gave each of them Coco Cola, and I gave each of them money to buy a treat. When no girls came to this meeting I learned from the boys that girls are not permitted to go out after dark so they could not come to our focus group.

A Different World

Ethiopian project focus group.

    The next afternoon, we had a meeting at the Ministry of Agriculture with our extension service counterpart. We found out what changes we would need to make in our 'Scope of Work.' The word "involved" is more important than "organization" for youth of co-ops. The Epiphany holiday began that afternoon. Our driver drove us around to see the beginning Epiphany festivities.

    The Epiphany holiday was the next day, and the mother and wife of the son of famous Jamaican singer Bob Marley were staying in the Hilton Hotel. I met them in the lobby at a morning coffee ceremony. The coffee beans were roasted first, then incense was put on coals to make an aroma. We all drank coffee together. Ethiopia claims to be the country where coffee originated.

    I watched the Epiphany Parade out of my hotel room window and saw the carrying of the Ark of the Covenant. I walked up the hill to St. Gabrielle's Church to see a celebration of the Ark of the Covenant. There was much chanting and sounds that were like American Indian whooping. Ethiopia claims to have the original Biblical Ark of the Covenant given by Solomon to his and Queen of Sheba's son who became King Menelek I of Ethiopia. The ark is now in a chapel at Axum next to the church of Mt. Mary of Zion. The chapel was constructed by Emperor Haile Selassie. Nobody is allowed to see the Ark of the Covenant at Axum that is said to be made of acacia wood overlaid with gold, and it contains the stone tablets of the Ten Commandments received from God by Moses on Mt. Sinai.

The next day, the Muslim holy day began at noon. My co-worker set up my laptop computer with his CD so I could read his papers about rural youth. I read the documents until my eyes tired, and I went to bed early. I spent another day putting together my gender issue ideas and a summary about rural youth in Ethiopia that would make a difference in the future organizing of their youth programs.

That weekend I read more of my co-worker's documents and we exchanged documents written on each other's discs. There was another large wedding breakfast in the hotel lobby and a lot of noise that we heard when the bride and groom arrived accompanied by a traditional drum and chanting corps.

The next week, a driver drove my co-worker and me to the Ministry of Agriculture and we had conferences with men that gave us the proceedings from a youth conference held a year earlier. We copied excerpts from it for our youth report. Fresh banana bread and fruit brought to my room daily by the maid helped prevent my taking breaks while I was writing on a laptop computer.

A Different World

An executive from our project organization national office in Washington, D.C., arrived and arrangements were made for all the staff to go to lunch together. It was an Ethiopian meal where all food is put on a big tray and everyone eats from the tray with their fingers. I ordered roasted beef on a little brazier and ate it by myself with a spoon. I did taste the teff served to all the others and it was flavorless though it had iron in it when it was made with red teff. Teff was broken into pieces and wrapped around other food to pick it up. I also tasted banana root squares that were bitter. Some of the staff added red pepper to their water to dip the food. Lunch ended with hot tea.

My co-worker and I had an afternoon appointment at Sasakawa-Global 2000 where we met the head of it that was an Ethiopian. It was an interesting one hour conference. We returned to our hotel to find we were both moved to different rooms.

The days that followed included writing a report for the Ethiopian Extension Service. My co-worker and I exchanged discs before completion of the final report. It took time to work on recommendations that would make a difference in their work. I added my workshop planning model to the gender issue paper. At the conclusion of my project about the women of Ethiopia, I recommended action should be taken to recognize Ethiopian rural women in extension program development, and women be taught to use agricultural technologies that would make a difference in their country.

My co-worker went over the recommendations I wrote, and we spent an hour of collaboration about both his and my work. 4-H Clubwork can develop methods for reaching out-of-school rural youth with a sustainable agriculture message. Programs can be accomplished and make a difference in Ethiopia through cooperation and collaboration among ministries in the government. 4-H Clubwork has been successful in many countries of the world because it is able to adapt to changing conditions.

I packaged several books to send to the focus group of boys we met with at Bahir Dar. We drove to the office for a conference with the program director and made an outline for our co-op final report. Work on that report was next. When I was finished with a section I took the disc to my co-worker for his approval, and to add to what he was writing.

The first of February the weather turned colder and the atmosphere hazy, so I could not see the mountains in the distance. The maid brought me guava fruit—green skin like a pomegranate, only a little bigger than a golf ball. It had pink flesh, soft and bright color with many little round white seeds. It grows on a big tree and was just in season, and was a new taste experience for me.

A driver took my co-worker and me to the office to turn in our second report, and the program officer was happy with it. The final report still needed to be written. The driver took us to the Haile Selassie store on Churchill Road for shopping before returning to the hotel. I sent my gender issue final report to USAID by driver who delivered it.

My final report writing took so much time the maid cleaned my room with me in it because I could not spare time required to write problems, recommendations, actions, and the anticipated impact of twenty recommendations to the two organizations of our project. I also wrote descriptions of the organizations for the report, and set up the form.

It was the first week in February, and the day of project debriefing, when the driver transported my co-worker and me to the Ministry of Agriculture for a conference about our draft report. We then went to the project office for a half hour debriefing with the East Africa representative and two others from his office. We were required to fill out two questionnaires for them. We then returned to the Hilton Hotel where we printed out our final reports and bound two with plastic binders.

The last day in Addis Ababa the driver took my co-worker and me on a mountain drive to see the scenery with many views of the city. Many people along the roads were carrying eucalyptus stripping to use for firewood.

The driver took me to Ethiopia's National Museum to see our ancestor "Lucy;" thirty-five million years old. A 1974 expedition discovered the fossil bones of Lucy, a female, small in stature—the short leg bones suggested a height of three and a half to four feet. She had cut her wisdom teeth, so she was grown when she died. The Beatles song "Lucy in the Sky with Diamonds" was popular at the time, and as the discoverers sat around one evening listening to the song someone said, "Why don't we call her Lucy?" She is also known as Denkenesh, an Ethiopian name meaning "You are wonderful"—her discovery marked a milestone in the study of mankind's prehistory.

"Lucy" is a partial skeleton, far more complete than anything found previously. Only in excavations dating to 100,000 years ago have comparably intact skeletons been unearthed. In viewing the remains of the skeleton, I learned that I was looking at reproduced bones as the originals are too fragile to be out in a glass case environment where people could view them.

It is thought "Lucy" walked upright along an Ethiopian lake shore. The crescent indentation on the inner edge of the pelvis bone tells her sex. The angle of the thigh bone and the flattened surface at its knee joint end—so different from quadrupedal apes—prove she walked on two legs. Not enough of the cranium survives to measure her brain size.

The museum also had interesting crowns and monarch garments, paintings, and artifacts. Then the driver drove me to the university to the former palace of Emperor Haile Selassie to see his bedroom, pastel blue bathroom, drawing room, gifts and clothes, and office building, the bedroom of his wife, and an Ethnography Museum. My working time in Ethiopia had come to an end.

CHAPTER 14
Mozambique, Africa

A twenty-two day project in Mozambique required me to fly to JFK, New York, followed by a South African Airways fourteen hour flight to Johannesburg, South Africa, where I connected with a flight to Maputo, Mozambique. Upon arrival my luggage did not arrive with me as there was too little transfer time between arrival in New York and my departure time on South African Airways. I filed a "luggage claim" right away and was told it would arrive the next day. I stayed overnight in Maputo's Hotel Cardoso and continued taking malaria medication the same as in all my days in African countries.

I rode the hotel shuttle the next morning to the airport to board LAM Linhas Aereas Airline for a flight to Beira. Everyone was aboard the plane when it was announced the airport was closed and everyone needed to vacate the plane. The prime minister of Portugal's plane was landing and a dignitary reception formed with a twenty-one gun salute, military band, and review of native dancers. One and one-half hours later we boarded the plane again for the one hour flight to Beira. A driver met me at the airport, and I again reported my "lost luggage" at the Beira Airport.

The driver took me to the home of the Beira chairman and she had lunch ready. I was given an afternoon tour of the Beira office, and I checked into Hotel Embaixador. That evening the Beira chairman and her husband came to the hotel and took me out for a seafood dinner. Her husband is a native Iowan from Henry County, and she is British.

The next morning a driver drove me from the hotel to the Beira office where a worker took me shopping to buy clothing that I needed with $100.00 of their office money: four blouses, one pair black slacks, one bra, one pantie, one pair nylon anklets. At noon we left the office to drive to a take-out lunch and from there drove on to Manica on rough roads, typical of Africa, and a few good roads.

It was more than three hours of fast driving before check-in at Manica's Hotel Pensao De Piscina. The room was Spartan—no closet or clothes hangers. I was told someone would meet me at 5 p.m. The consul's wife was on the hotel terrace and said it would be her husband, though he was working late in the field. She took me to her home, only two houses from the hotel, but the consul did not come home that day so I returned to my hotel room.

I was awakened at 2 a.m. when dogs barked outside my window; at 3 a.m. ants crawled on me and I could no longer sleep. Birds began singing at 5 a.m. Roosters crowed at 5:30 a.m. I went back to sleep at 6 a.m. and was awake and to breakfast at 7:30 a.m.

The consul's driver took me to his office. The consul and a translator arrived before noon and we drove to a village field where the consul had camped overnight with his brother-in-law and an elderly man. They had six servings of barbecued chicken, vegetables and greasy fries, but I declined eating lunch on mats on the ground remembering medical advice. We returned to Manica for tea at the consul's home. I then went to the hotel restaurant for hot vegetable soup.

Rain began in the night. Ants crawled on my forehead and in one of my ears. The next morning I went to the hotel desk and requested that I be moved to a different room. That same day I moved to a room that had recently been painted and cleaned.

I walked to the American Friends Service in a home one block from the hotel where the project director turned on a computer and set it up so I could write emails home to my family so they would know of my arrival. The consul was not coming to his office until late. While I was eating a hot beef dinner in the hotel restaurant, the consul came to my table to conference with me for half an hour about plans for the next day. He wanted to dry ginger, a plentiful crop that had export potential.

Nights became cooler and I slept with all the blankets in my room. I walked to the consul's office on Saturday morning, and he filled his four-wheel-drive vehicle with his family and me, and picked up my translator to drive to Chimanyha Messica Villa Carpentry Shop to consult on construction of a solar dryer. My translator was certified at a woodworking school.

We then drove to Lake Chicamba that was formed by a large dam. We saw mountain scenery and many villages along the way. I saw a man plowing with oxen and a walking plow. The consul left me with my translator at noon to sit around a table by the lake, under a thatched hut roof, while he and his family went to their farm. They returned later with chicken and fish to cook and a salad. I refrained from eating and waited to eat hot food at the hotel.

My second week in the office I was included with my translator in a staff session of eight other people. They turned over one hour of the conference to me to explain and discuss my project that would make a difference in food preparation using a solar dryer. I walked back to the hotel for lunch at noon. The consul transported me to his office for afternoon work on word processing several pages for the manual I planned to use with the solar dryer.

Staff meeting in Mozambique.

The Beira office phoned that my luggage had arrived at the Beira Airport. It was the next day before a Beira driver arrived with my luggage while I was working on my project manual pages in the consul's office. I returned to the hotel and unpacked my luggage, and sorted the dried fruit samples in it that had traveled from Oregon in good condition. I listened to my short wave radio that evening.

Some days I walked from the hotel to the consul's office, and sometimes he came along and picked me up to drive the remainder of the way. My translator gave me a report of the slow progress on the building of the solar dryer. I continued working on additional pages for my manual and made three copies. Two copies were for the country director. My translator cut grass to be used for insulation in the solar dryer, but the wood construction still needed to be finished.

Daylight grew longer with each passing day. Mozambique is south of the equator.

A worker took me one day from the consul's office to the nearby school to see classrooms and all the other buildings. A teacher of five and six year old children had fifty-two students. She spoke very good English and told me about their daily schedule. The remainder of the time I set up my final report outline on the office computer.

While the solar dryer neared completion, my translator talked with me about his tribal cultural marriage traditions and his family history. The consul joined in the conversation about native religions and culture, then drove us to the Messica Carpentry Shop to see the solar dyer progress. I was shocked to see the size of it. It took four men to lift it. It still needed paint and holes drilled in it and a lid. I requested they remake one tray that was short and would allow heat to escape to the cover without penetrating the fruit. My interpreter stayed at the shop to work on the dryer. I returned with the consul to his office. I met with the consul and with the committee for acquiring fruit and supplies for my demonstration. It started to rain and continued to rain off and on all weekend.

Solar dryer.

Saturday I was invited to the consul's daughter's birthday party that included their extended family and the consul's colleagues. The carport was decorated and the children wore party hats, played games, and danced all afternoon. The men played soccer in the driveway. I met the head of Chimoio Health Alliance International, another USAID funded program. A woman was present from another health organization and said cholera had broken out in Beira again with one death; unusual before the rainy season.

Sunday afternoon my translator made arrangements to meet me and walk to the market where all the used clothing shipped to Mozambique from USA was offered for sale. It was sorted and hung up for easy access to buyers. None of the clothing was given free-of-charge to needy

Mozambique country residents, even though it was the poorest country in the world at that time.

The third week I was in the consul's office, the Africare director from Chimoio arrived to see the solar dryer and discussed with me the possibility of making a basket dryer for the use of poor natives in his area.

The two days of my fruit drying demonstration there was beautiful, clear-sky weather. The goal of my demonstration was to make a difference in the nutrition of the people and utilize the abundance of fruit in season. The first day I walked to the consul's office at 7 a.m. My translator was already there and had already moved the solar dryer to the demonstration area. I went to the demonstration area and people began arriving.

That morning I gave my introduction speech and it was translated to twenty-eight people consisting of seventeen women and eleven men. A farmer came to me and said he would bring strawberries to dry the second day. I demonstrated oranges, orange rind, and pineapple, and told of the importance of adding them to the diet. My translator helped me set up an assembly line of women to prepare enough fruit to fill the two large trays that fit into the solar dryer.

The temperature in the solar dryer registered 60 C. degrees when I put orange slices in at 11:15 a.m. and it reached 70 C. degrees by 12:05 noon for the pineapple. That was the correct temperature for two hours. That afternoon clouds from the Zimbabwe mountains moved in and thunder could be heard. The sun kept breaking through the clouds.

The group ate lunch together, consuming rice and boiled maize with fish stew and goat meat. I gave the group samples of all the dried foods I brought with me from USA. I summarized the demonstration, and my translator translated what I said in summary in the Portuguese language so it could be understood by those in attendance.

The second demonstration day the driver picked me up at the hotel and drove me to the solar dryer area. All morning, until noon, I demonstrated the drying of sliced papaya, strawberries, and bananas. I gave a summary of the demonstration that was translated so the group could understand my explanations. The weather was warmer, but the oranges and pineapple from the first day were not completely dry. The group again ate lunch together, and all the staff at the consul's office came to the demonstration area to join in the lunch. I ate with them as all the food was hot and there was no left over food from lunch the first day.

The consul made a video of my first workshop day demonstrations and everyone went to his office in the afternoon of the second day to view the video. The consul asked me to make recommendations and give a summary. My translator again translated everything I said. I was overwhelmed by all the "Thank You" speeches given to me that followed my presentation, and their singing "have courage to dry fruit" and their chant: "This is what the American brought us."

That afternoon I was interviewed by the local radio station using a translator. Later, that evening there were flashes of lightning, then thunder so loud it was impossible to sleep. At midnight the rain poured and there was a four-hour storm. Electricity in the hotel went off. I heard loud Portuguese language talk of men and women in the hallway during the storm. The rainy season had definitely started.

The floor of my room was filled with dead termites when I awakened the next morning. After breakfast, I walked part way and then a driver picked me up to take me to the consul's office. I spent the time on the computer to input final report revisions until the office staff had tea time with omelets and bread. It became my meal for the day. That afternoon my translator and a worker in the consul's office met me at the hotel to solicit help from me about a grant of money they applied for to Global Fund for Women, Palo Alto, California. I talked with them about it.

The next day at the consul's office I transferred my final report onto a disc. Arrangements were made for my travel to Chimoio. The consul's wife gave me a Mozambique cookbook, and I listened to news on my short wave radio. It was overcast and cooler, definitely not a day to use a solar dryer.

My last weekend in Manica I walked to the Christian Church and went in to listen to the singing and drum music. The church was completely full of people. I shook a lot of hands and walked with people to the cemetery where many were placing flowers on the graves.

Later that day, I went with the consul and his wife to the Messica River where it is dammed and we drove through a lot of brush to a lovely farm of one hundred hectares where herbs and vegetables grow. Chicken was barbecued and beef sausage served with fresh baked bread. I did not eat the salad. We stayed until dark, walking to the water's edge, and sat on huge granite boulders to watch the colorful sunset until time to return to Manica.

Africare's director arrived at my Manica hotel early the next day to transport me to Chimoio. The consul's family came to the hotel to bid me "goodbye."

It was a two hour and fifteen minute drive to Chimoio. We went immediately to the Africare office and I was introduced to the staff. There were twenty-six staff members, though some were in the field. Before lunch that morning we washed oranges, mangoes, papaya, tomatoes and three kinds of dry leaves. The director took me to his home for lunch where I met his wife, a trained nurse, and women from Sweden and Zimbabwe with whom his wife was working. The afternoon return to Africare's office was met with many staff questions about use of a basket for drying. Later that day, we took fruit to the director's home to dry it in the oven. It had started to rain.

I stayed overnight in the home of the Africare director and his wife. There was mosquito netting over my bed, and I took my first shower with hot water. Maputo Hotel showers had only cold water.

I had an early drive the next morning with the director of Africare to his office. I held a fruit drying summary and set solar baskets out in the sun with oranges, mangoes, tomatoes, rind, peaches, and papaya. When it was lunch time we returned to the director's home. That afternoon we went to the Africare office to check on the solar baskets. The fruit and tomatoes needed turning and were not done on the underside. Leaves and rind were finished drying. That evening the director's cook made a delicious dinner and served South African liqueur. I played several games of Scrabble that evening with the director and his wife until bedtime.

The next morning a driver came from Beira to transport me from Chimoio to Beira's Hotel Embaixador where I had stayed earlier. I caught up on sending emails. Early the next day the driver transported me to the office for my debriefing. Later that morning, the driver showed me the beach area before returning me to the hotel for lunch. The driver returned in the afternoon to take me on a tour of the port. The next day I was transported to the Beira Airport for a flight to Maputo that arrived at noon.

I flew one hour to Johannesburg, South Africa, and rode a hotel shuttle to the Airport Holiday Inn, a beautiful hotel. I went on a USA $55.00 tour to Soweto that departed my hotel at 10:30 a.m. Soweto is a poor city. Its largest

A Different World

black township had four million people at that time. I toured President Nelson and Winnie Mandela's home, then saw where she was living at the time I was there. I also saw where Bishop Tutu lived. The tour stopped at Nunki Catholic Church, the largest in South Africa, and drove slowly past Chris Hani Baragwanath Hospital which is the largest on the African continent where thirty-five thousand babies are born each year.

The tour of Johannesburg's Museum of Africa I had was interesting, especially the gold exhibit, and a squatter's shambles house. The tour then drove to a viewpoint of the city. Johannesburg has no big rivers, dams, no ocean, not even a big mountain. The size of Greater Johannesburg was two hundred miles, altitude 1,763 meters, almost as high as Mexico City. I shopped at the flea market and bought two ostrich eggs, one carved and one etched, that I had never seen before in any country.

The next morning I had an 8:15 a.m. boarding time for a South African Airlines flight to Cape Verde Sal Island in the Atlantic Ocean. The crew changed because it was another seven hours flying time to JFK, New York. Then I had flights to Atlanta, Georgia, Salt Lake City, and Portland, Oregon before arrival home to meet my husband on the day of our 42nd wedding anniversary.

Margaret Krug Palen

CHAPTER 15
Belarus, European Project

My fifteen-day volunteer project in Belarus began with a non-stop flight from Oregon to Atlanta, Georgia, and then to Munich, Germany, with a connecting Lufthansa Airline flight to Minsk, Belarus. There is a ten hour difference in time between my home and Belarus.

The country director and the project development/ evaluator specialist met me at the airport to drive twenty-six miles to a Minsk hotel located across from the post office. The hotel covered a whole city block with an entrance on Independence Square, where Lenin's statue was still in front of the parliament building. The hammer and sickle was still on buildings, and I was told it was the symbol of the Soviet Union and not Russia. Belarusians think that symbol is historic. My first impression was Belarus is a city of large buildings.

The country director checked me in at the hotel and walked me to his office to leave the herb seeds and hazelnut coffee I was requested to bring with me. We returned to the hotel and Igor, my translator, was waiting in the lobby to meet me. The director briefed us on a schedule for the next day.

The next morning my translator, Igor, met me early in the hotel lobby, and I rushed to check out of the hotel. We caught a taxi to the train depot and boarded a first-class coach where the attendant brought hot tea and biscuits.

Our train departure was at 7:48 a.m. with arrival in Bobryuisk at 10:15 a.m. Our host was a half hour late meeting us because he thought arrival would be at the other train station in the city of 225,000 population and three technical institutions.

It was an hour drive to the village of Slavkovichy, a "dying village" in the Magyler Region. The host's wife, with the help of a neighbor lady, had lunch ready that was more like a dinner and served with champagne and chocolates. I did not eat the salad. The host then drove my translator, Igor, and me to his fifty hectares of herbs. Returning to the host's home I went for a walk in the "dying village" to see vacant houses and a memorial to those who died in World War II. We were served a large dinner that evening with peach liqueur and more chocolates. I showed the host family photos of my family which they liked. There was no inside plumbing in the host's house, only an outdoor toilet.

The next day my translator, Igor, went jogging with me and exercised before breakfast. I conferenced that morning with the host about his herb production and his problems; that assisted my understanding of the help he needed.

A driver from the Belarus office arrived just before lunch which was more like a dinner menu. Then it was time to leave the "dying village," and as I was directed, I gave the host's wife $20.00 USA which she would cash on the Black Market and get multi-million rubles for it. I wanted to give her more, but my translator, Igor, said, "No."

We drove seven hours north to Zaborye, a village in the Vitebsk Region, Shumilino District, to the home of a farmer that had been in the herb business for five years. He had a sauna going and dinner was served at 10:30 p.m. An outdoor toilet had no seat in it and was impossible for me to use. The next morning, my translator, Igor, saw me outdoors early, and joined me to walk on the paved road a short distance past the farmer's home to a forested area where he explained the deep holes in the forest floor were from bombs by German troops in World War II. He suggested I crawl into that area and use it for a toilet, which I did the remainder of the time I was in that village.

The farmer took my translator, Igor, and me on a tour of his farm machinery lot and herb drying shed. He and two other farmers had been independent of government farming since the 1990's when Russia became bankrupt. They were given a bank loan and bought their own machinery. He showed us his large potato combine, wheat combine, tractors and trucks. He was an electrical engineer and built his own sawmill and demonstrated it by cutting four boards at once. He designed his own cross-saw, flour mill, and plainer, and demonstrated them. He was drying valerian root. His motherwort was crushed and sacked, and his chamomile was also crushed and sacked. He sold it to a pharmaceutical company in Vitebsk.

That afternoon the farmer took Igor and me to see his fields of motherwort and his new plantings of chamomile and valerian. It was the first time I saw beggarticks (Bidens frondosa) growing. In late afternoon we drove to a lake and went out on a raft from 5-7 p.m. The farmer caught four perch fish, and stopped at a pond to put the fish in it before we returned to his home for a late dinner.

Margaret inspecting plants with a Belarus farmer.

A Different World

I was awake at 6 a.m. and walked down the village road to the forest to use it again for a toilet. While waiting that morning for a driver to come for us, my translator, Igor, walked with me to the village streets and we talked with women that we met that were hunting mushrooms. When the driver arrived he had a Belarus herb businessman with him, and we drove to a farm that produced herbs for the businessman. We looked at dill, lavage, and coriander (cilantro). There were many weeds in the fields. Then we drove to a village to see the new administration building the businessman was building, and we went to his factory that was small and substandard. We returned to Minsk that evening.

The next morning I ate a buffet breakfast in the Minsk Hotel before I walked to the Saturday market, but there was nothing there that interested me. I returned to the office and worked on my reports until my translator, Igor, arrived and he walked me to several places where he thought there might be lace, but we did not find any lace. I bought four Russian paper lacquered boxes to take home to my family. Igor and I rode in a taxi to the train station that evening for an 11:25 p.m. departure in a sleeper car.

A train attendant knocked on my compartment door at 6 a.m. Arrival in Grodno was at 7: 05 a.m. The Bio-Test Herb Company driver was there to drive us to Hotel Grodno. Igor did not like the hotel and asked the driver to take us to a tourist hotel. Later, the driver drove us to the home of a retired military man who had turned farmer. He joined us and we picked up his daughter, a Russian language teacher, and drove more miles to the farmer's buckthorn plantation.

We looked at the farmer's buckthorn and then the men built a fire and his daughter picked buckthorn berries with me. The farmer put the berries through a food chopper to juice them, and added vodka to make a cocktail. They opened up a picnic basket filled with a large amount of food including meat pies. We danced around the fire after the potatoes baked and ate a large meal, but I did not drink any of the vodka cocktail. It was an hour drive through terrible roads to tour an old castle, and the old part of the city of Grodno. We returned to the hotel that evening.

The next morning we drove to Bio-Test Administrative offices to meet the director and staff and attend a conference until noon. The director wanted to buy the herb reference book I had with me, but I could not sell it because I borrowed it in Oregon for the project and had to return it. Lunch was at a Belarus State Restaurant. In the afternoon we drove to a bio-test pharmacy where I saw herbs sold, also prescription medicines. Some of the packaged herbs were from Poland. We visited a three hundred year old pharmacy museum.

We returned to the bio-test factory to see the packaging and shipping of huge sacks of herbs that were larger than I have ever seen. I had a conference with the director about buying forty-three kinds of herbs from farmers. We departed at 5 p.m. to walk by the river and castle. Then the driver drove my translator, Igor, and me to the bio-test director's home where his wife served us "herring under fur coat" (beet and mayonnaise-covered chopped herring) dinner with wine. The driver drove us to a 10 p.m. train departure to return to Minsk.

The next morning I went to the office and worked on a computer until my translator, Igor, arrived. We went over the slide pictures I planned to show the next day at the opening herb seminar. The remainder of the day I worked on my program for the seminar, and also spent the evening studying herb material to use for the seminar.

The next morning, I saw the room where the herb seminars were to be held for the first time, and I helped set it up. There were seventeen herb farmers, two staff, and my translator, Igor, in attendance. A resource person, who was planned in advance, made the first presentation. Then it was my turn to show a slide presentation of herb growing in USA, and I had feedback about it that showed the differences in growing some of the same herbs in USA and in Belarus. Noon lunch was at a Belarus State Restaurant. The World Bank paid for the lunch and gave each seminar participant money for their evening dinner, and also paid their hotel bill. The afternoon program was a division into discussion groups to bring out herb problems in need of being addressed.

The second day, the herb seminar's first resource presenter was the son of the bio-test director we met in Grodno. He was a university student and answered questions following his presentation. The next presenter was the businessman who operated an herb factory, and who we had met in Vitebsk. He had just returned from Moscow and his presentation was very interesting. There was time for cluster group discussions and feedback before adjourning for lunch at the same state restaurant.

In the afternoon a bus picked up all the seminar participants to drive outside the city limits, a twenty-five minute drive, to a seventeen-hectare herb garden with six hectares of ginseng owned by one of the seminar attendees. Many of the herbs were brought from Asia and the East, and I had never ever seen them. The seminar closed when we returned to the meeting rooms, and each person attending received the herb seeds I brought from USA, and a staff member raffled off five books about herbs. The seminar closed that afternoon with coffee and tea.

The next day was my last day in the Belarus office. That morning I finished my final report and gave it to the director. He preferred the computer report be put on a disc. We walked to the Ministry of Agriculture buffet lunch, and I paid for the director and his assistant's lunch. That afternoon I filled out several evaluation forms before leaving the office.

The afternoon was spent visiting the Minsk Museum with a guide, a university teacher who had been arranged to take me around the city. We were in the museum an hour, and then walked to the Russian Orthodox Cathedral. We went to the subway entrance where fifty-three young people died in May of that year trying to get inside from the rain and they trampled each other to death, a tragedy that I had heard about in the worldwide news. At a state store I looked for blue and white dishes and bought a lovely dish for my daughter.

My last day in Belarus was Sunday, and the same university guide arranged to meet me in the afternoon to walk to the old city houses and "island of tears." It was a memorial for the Afghanistan War. We walked to the National Academic Grand Opera and Ballet Theatre of the Republic of Belarus and Victory Square for World War II, then rode the metro to the Botanical Gardens for a tour. I bought my granddaughter a flax doll to add to her collection. The day together ended at my hotel.

I checked out of the Belarus Hotel to be at the Belarus Airport for a Lufthansa Airline flight to Frankfurt, Germany. I bought a train ticket to Marburg where Edda Simon, the Löhlbach forester's wife, met me and drove me to Löhlbach, to my cousin Marlene Boehle's home where I stayed that night and for two days.

It was good to be in my ancestral village again. The next morning I went for a walk in the village and rejoiced in seeing it again. The Löhlbach church pastor came that afternoon and drove me to Willie Hackel's home, the person who researched my genealogy, and we went to Huttingen where we visited the church of the village that dates to 900 A.D. We stopped in the cemetery to visit the grave of my

A Different World

fourth cousin's husband whom I had met on an earlier year visit to their home. We drove to my cousin's home and her son and wife and two children arrived. Her son spoke English and interpreted for us. We stopped at Willie's son's nearby farm to meet him, and then returned to my cousin Marlene's Löhlbach home.

The second day of this visit in Löhlbach, I again went for a morning walk on the streets of the village where houses my ancestors had lived in were familiar to me. My cousin Marlene took me to see the renovated Krug house #70 where my great-grandfather was born. That day I met Paar relatives of my Great-Great Grandmother Krug. I walked to the cemetery to visit the grave of my Krug 4th cousin whom I met the last time I was in Löhlbach, and had since died. In the afternoon I went to the village forester, Hermann Simon's home for tea and cakes on their patio and a tour of Edda's pottery studio. That evening I was invited to dinner at the home of my genealogy researcher and I realized, after more time had elapsed, that was the last time I saw him and his wife whom he also found in my family genealogy. The next morning, Marlene drove me to Marburg to board the train to Frankfurt Main, and a ride on another train to the airport for my airline flight to Atlanta, Georgia, and a non-stop flight to return to my Oregon home.

Margaret Krug Palen

A Different World

CHAPTER 16
Bolivia, South America

My month in South America began with airline flights to Chicago's O' Hare Airport, and Miami, Florida. I made lace on my travel pillow on the long flight to La Paz, capital city of Bolivia. There were beautiful views of the Andes Mountains from the plane windows. The airplane was overloaded and could not take off from La Paz El Alto International Airport, one of the two highest airports in the world at elevation 13,323 feet, until it was unloaded. After a two hour delay we landed in Santa Cruz, and I missed my flight to Tarija, Bolivia.

In Santa Cruz, I was met by a program representative and taken to the House Inn Hotel which is all apartments. The country director phoned me twice at the hotel about the next day's schedule. I had a morning conference with the country director before my flight to Sucre and on to Tarija over very mountainous country.

There was nobody to meet me at the airport. I rode in a taxi to Hostal Costanera, a bed and breakfast on a boulevard. I phoned the local office and it was 5:30 p.m. before anyone came to meet me with a translator from the British Embassy. My counterpart could only speak Spanish and walked me to the office to give me a quick look at it.

I listened to English language news on TV in my room the next morning before a breakfast of an abundance of fresh fruit and juices; more than I had ever had at breakfast in any country: strawberries, avocado, papaya, pineapple, bananas, and several kinds of grapes. Then I walked to the office and two Peace Corps interpreters waited to translate my counterpart's Spanish for me.

We went to my counterpart's workroom to be shown dried tomatoes, potatoes, onions, garlic, peas and his experiments with color and blanching. He invited us to his home for lunch that was served by his mother: peanut soup with floating French fries and beer, a full plate of green noodles topped with chicken and beef, tomato sauce and shredded cheese. The dessert was several kinds of grapes.

That afternoon there was a conference about my Plan of Work. I gave my counterpart a potato soup mix sample I brought from Oregon, and showed him photos of my Mozambique solar dryer and the manual to go with it that was translated into Portuguese.

The next day, when I arrived at the office, my counterpart was cleaning out a large dehydrator of oregano and chamomile. I drove with my counterpart and a Peace Corps translator in a truck; one hour on a very rough road to Selle Las Quebrads. We met for an hour with women that process peaches. One hundred families and twenty women do the processing and they market all of the peaches. In another room goat cheese was made. A wedge of cheese was cut off for each of us to taste. Then it was a sharp, downhill walk to the gardens and orchards to see where the peaches grow. Walnuts were being gathered to eat green, and to make into soup. I gave all the women ballpoint pens I had been instructed to take to Bolivia with me for local gifts. The women gave me apples and a jar of peaches that I gave to my hostel owner when I returned there that evening.

At the end of my first week it was time to draft a Plan of Work and fax it to the Santa Cruz office. I conferred with my counterpart about it. He spent the day preparing oregano that had dried eight hours on forty trays in a gas dehydrator.

A Different World

At coffee break we ate hot pastries called Empanadas that were filled with ground beef, potato cubes and onions. They were delicious with an orange drink.

The first weekend in Tarija I walked to the Museum of Paleontology. I have never seen so many fossils with huge jawbones and teeth. All were from Bolivia 250,000 years ago. Also, I saw the largest armadillo skeleton I have ever seen. There was a lot of pottery and arrow heads, and grinding stones of various Indian tribes such as the San Blas. One room was filled with minerals from Bolivia mines near Sucre and Potosi.

I walked to the Casa de la Cultura home of Moises Navajas Ichazo and Esperanza, his wife, wealthy importers of European merchandise sold in Bolivia and Argentina. They built a palace in sixteen years and lived in it fifty years. It had been vacant thirty years when I visited it. The music concert room had a Steinway piano that had been played by Franz Liszt. A guide in the room played the piano for me. There was Louis XV furniture in the reception room. The chapel was beautiful.

It began to rain with lightning and thunder on the weekend, and continued for two more days. Monday my translator worked with me to process tomatoes—scalding, blanching, putting them in cold water and peeling them, and I showed my counterpart how to do it to make a difference in the finished product. He put large trays of tomatoes in the dehydrator at 5 p.m. Tuesday morning the tomatoes in the dehydrator were still not dry. The dehydrator shut off during the night and there were pools of water on the floor. That afternoon I had a conference with my counterpart about solar dryer models. He was interested in four of them, and he wanted construction details from me.

That week we drove across a mountain range on the road to Sucre. It was foggy driving on a high ledge road, and we crossed a long farming valley to start up another mountain range on a rocky road. It was ninety-five kilometers from Tarija to San Luis de Palqui. We arrived at noon and visited a garlic drying center to observe the village dehydrator and its screens.

A native woman of the village presented me with a gift sack of garlic. We went to lunch in an adobe house. I again gave out ballpoint pens to the locals. The children had arrow heads to sell and I bargained to buy several from them.

A Different World

The Bolivia project.

That afternoon I walked to a river and irrigation ditches where the men and native girls were catching two pounds of crayfish. Fortunately, I had packed my Bergmann boots, bought in my youth to climb Mt. Hood, and I needed them on this day. We returned to Tarija through a valley of cactus-covered mountains and rough road. We stopped for photos with the cactus.

The next day, when I returned to the office to check the dehydrator, I found the tomatoes were still drying. I spent the morning with my counterpart discussing the translation of my drying manual into Spanish so he could use it with workers in the communities that we visited. The remainder of my time was spent working on my reports, and I took the tomatoes out of the dehydrator after thirty six hours of drying. They were in the dehydrator a total of seventy-two hours, but not continuous heat because of the electricity failure.

My counterpart and I prepared squash all the mornings of the next week to put in the dehydrator. I spent time typing and editing my report.

That weekend I walked up the Avenue of the Americas and crossed the bridge to the high point of the city to see Bolivia's hero, Moto Mendez, on a horse statue. There were excellent views of the city from that point. Then the electricity went out in my hostel, and I listened to my short wave radio and used a flashlight. A loud lightning and thunder storm wakened me and continued into the week. When I arrived at the office my counterpart was drying out the dehydrator again as it had water in it from the rain storms. He took the squash out and it was not completely dry, and it had to be put back in when the dehydrator was ready again.

I worked on the computer and made pages to put in my final report. My counterpart boiled potatoes and dried them in the dehydrator. That day my translator, my counterpart, and I stripped anise from two large bags brought in by the women and children that had picked it. Anise grows wild when the rains begin. By noon, one half of one bag was ready for screens to go into the dehydrator. It takes six hours for anise to dry. That afternoon was spent stripping more anise, but we did not finish it until another day. The anise that was put in the dehydrator earlier came out in a dry condition.

With my translator's assistance, I discussed the forty page manual my counterpart had to train workers on sanitation and safety in preparing food for preservation work. My counterpart did the drawing and layout. I gave him information on vegetable drying to make it into a technical manual.

It was still raining on Thursday of my third week in Tarija. My counterpart helped me put my final report on a disc. That afternoon the administrator and his wife grilled a beef and sausage barbecue at the office and served it with white wine as a "farewell" meal for me. The office accountant and coordinator joined us to eat. When "goodbyes" were said my translator left and I walked back to Hostal Costanera.

Friday morning of my last week in Tarija I walked to the office and the staff had two commemorative leather souvenirs of remembrance to present to me. I was also given a document to deliver to the Santa Cruz Country director. My flight to Santa Cruz was delayed, and my counterpart taxied me to the airport and waited with me until the Bolivian Airlines plane departed for Santa Cruz.

In Santa Cruz I conferenced with the county director, and he suggested I see Machu Picchu before returning to USA. He sent his secretary with me to a travel agent to get tickets for a flight to Cusco, Peru. I flew the next morning from the airport and saw a large Andes peak before landing at La Paz El Alto International Airport. The flight over Lake Titicaca was long and I could realize the largeness of it; it is South America's highest lake at 12,500 feet above sea level.

Cusco's Alejandro Velasco Astete International Airport is almost seventy-five miles from Machu Picchu and the city is high in the Andes, more than 11,000 feet above sea level. It was the center of the vast Inca Empire in the 15th and 16th centuries. The arrival of conquistadors in 1533 changed all that. The Spanish quickly laid siege to the city's riches, squatted there briefly, then moved on to the coast and the newly formed colonial capital of Lima.

I was told ahead of time that in Cusco I would see people selling coca leaves, and also see people chewing them. I saw plastic bags jammed full of the green leaves and I saw men walking down the streets with cheeks puffed out, gnawing on wads of coca leaves thought to alleviate altitude sickness. I learned cocaine is processed from coca leaves. I was not concerned with altitude sickness as I had been at elevations of 11,000 feet and more a number of times while climbing in the Cascade Mountains, and I also have been to 14,115 foot Pikes Peak in Colorado and I have never suffered from the altitude.

I walked the cobble-stoned streets of Cusco to the Plaza de Armas and visited the cathedral. I sat for minutes observing a wedding taking place in front of the altar. I walked around the plaza and came to a woman sitting on the sidewalk, and up against a building, with her feet outstretched to which she had warp threads attached from her toes to her waistline to form a loom. She was weaving. This brought back my memory of my Iowa State University historic textiles professor teaching that it was still possible to see women in South and Central America hand-weaving using their feet and waistlines for a loom. I took a photograph of the Cusco weaver.

Hand-weaving using feet and waistlines for a loom

I checked into the Royal Palace Hostel and walked to the nearby travel agent office to buy a package tour to Machu Picchu. Then I shopped Cusco's market streets and found prices were high so I returned to the hostel for the night.

The next morning I had a continental breakfast before the tour company picked me up for the drive to the train station for a 6 a.m. train departure. The train slowly wound around sixty-eight miles through the farming Sacred Valley with eighteen train switch-backs that each put the train on a higher elevation. At 9:20 a.m. I arrived in Aguas Calientes to board a bus to ride a half hour up very steep switchbacks on a mountain road. The scary, sharp road turns climbed higher and higher in elevation to reach Machu Picchu, the "Lost City of the Incas."

Built in the 15th century, Machu Picchu sits on a ridge atop jarring, steep mountains and was "discovered" by Hiram Bingham in 1911, and accorded a UNESCO World Heritage status in 1983. I joined a 10 a.m. guided tour of the Inca Empire ruins. It rained off and on during the tour, and I was thankful for having taken my umbrella. I ate food brought with me for lunch. I took a few photos in the afternoon when the sun came out. I wondered about theories as to why Machu Picchu existed: to determine winter or summer solstice, or for human sacrifice, or astronomical readings, or possibly to house precious gems. I looked around Machu Picchu before returning by bus to Aguas Calientes where I had reservations for overnight at a quaint hotel. My room was Spartan, and I walked the dirt roads of the village to find something to eat before going early to bed.

The next day, I got up at daylight and bought another bus ticket for Machu Picchu. I took the first bus back up the half hour ride of many switchbacks and scary straight down glimpses out of the bus window to return to Machu Picchu in brilliant sunshine. I again toured the site, especially the areas where it rained on my tour the previous day, and I walked in the Inca ruins before all the tours arrived for the day. I climbed higher up in the ruins than the tour went the previous day. There were three llamas in the ruins, and there was sunshine for taking more photos than the previous day.

Margaret at Machu Picchu.

I sat on the Machu Picchu Hotel veranda and enjoyed the views from there of the ruins. I wandered around Machu Picchu before returning to Aguas Calientes by train to ride back to Cusco to the same Royal Palace hotel where I had earlier stayed.

The next morning I took a taxi to Cusco's Alejandro Velasco Astete International Airport for my airplane departure. I arrived in La Paz El Alto International Airport and returned to Oregon via Miami, Florida, and Texas.

Margaret Krug Palen

CHAPTER 17
Jamaica, West Indies

My next project to make a difference in the world was three weeks in Jamaica, West Indies. It was another international project that addressed the most pressing and intractable development problems in food security.

Airline flights were from Oregon to Dallas/Ft. Worth and Florida to Kingston, Jamaica. The Airport Security in Jamaica took me to Tourist Information when there was nobody to meet me in Kingston. I gave them the cell phone number of the representative who planned to meet me and discovered he was already on the airport grounds, and he finally arrived to meet me. I exchanged USA dollars for Jamaican money because the Sandhurst Hotel where I would stay did not have facilities for doing it. The hotel was old and my room was very humid when I arrived. I watched TV before going to bed when lightning and thunder began, and it poured rain.

The next morning, I phoned the USA embassy to give them my next address at HighGate, Jamaica. At 9 a.m. a driver and van came to pick me up. Roads had many curves until arrival at HighGate Dolls and Crafts Ltd. where a seminar was in progress and I joined the sixteen people and five small children. I was requested to introduce myself and to speak to the group as adviser to a project of the HighGate Dolls and Craft Factory. Two women from Kingston presented a program about labeling and packaging of products. I learned the European Union had paid for the building of the kitchen in the HighGate Dolls and Craft Factory where my project would be the first to use the new kitchen.

It was my job to provide technical assistance in home economics skills and business enterprise to the HighGate Dolls and Crafts factory employees. It included, but was not limited to, creating with the members value-added coconut products to be utilized in training members in product development and formulation documentation. It also was my job to train workers in food product preservation and in quality control standards.

Later that afternoon, I was transported to a school teacher's home, supposedly within walking distance of the HighGate Dolls and Crafts Factory. I unpacked in the bedroom assigned to me that was not convenient. It was Wednesday and there was no water or electricity on that day each week. Dinner that evening was with her two sons, age ten and seventeen years. Shortly after eating, friends of the teacher came and took the two of us to a building where the teacher taught a Bible study once a week. Her teaching was Pentecostal with long prayers and singing. At 10 p.m. we returned to the teacher's home.

The next morning, after breakfast, I walked, with briefcase in hand, a mile that had a hill to climb from the teacher's home to HighGate Dolls and Crafts Factory. I was on a slow computer the first two hours of the day. Then I had a planning session with the manager and three women that were to work with me in the kitchen every day. I did not have any lunch, and no arrangements were made for it.

The factory manager left for the day at noon, and I walked across the road to the location of a Quaker Friends School and met the manager and his wife; the nephew and wife of a Salem man who told me about them when he learned I was going to Jamaica. They invited me to stay with them while I was working on my project. My supervisor came while I was at the Friends School and arrangements were made for me to stay with the teacher one week, and then move to the Friends School manager's home the second week. My supervisor gave me a ride back to the teacher's home that day.

Roosters began crowing early the next morning and they awakened me. The teacher's seventeen year old son cooked breakfast: delicious banana fritters and scrambled eggs. After breakfast I started walking to HighGate Dolls and Crafts Factory. As I arrived at a street corner, a HighGate kitchen coordinator ran out to meet me and gave me the keys to open the factory door. It took a while for me to get through all the padlocked doors and gates.

I worked on the computer until 11 a.m. when the production manager and several workers arrived making it possible for me to conduct a record keeping session with them. The factory manager arrived at 2 p.m. and the production manager left to buy lunch for me.

They liked the coconut doll and gourd design I brought with me to give them ideas and gifts for them from Oregon. That day I walked the distance to the teacher's home at the end of my work, and that evening mosquito netting was finally brought to cover my bed. I already had many mosquito bites.

The first weekend the teacher and her two sons slept until 10 a.m. I got up earlier and walked down the road in the opposite direction, and returned again to the teacher's house before anyone arose for the day. At 10:45 a.m. the teacher's oldest son started breakfast. Rain began to pour again. The youngest son did not get up until 11 a.m. I sprayed my room and clothes for mosquitoes as many came in when it rained.

My host teacher took me with her by bus to the town of HighGate. We grocery shopped at the farmers market and purchased vegetables. Her sister and brother-in-law drove us back to her home that afternoon. It continued raining off and on all day. We spent the evening looking at photos of the teacher's family, and of her 24-25 year old sister who won a silver medal in the Sydney, Australia, 2000 Olympics, and planned to go for the world title to qualify for the next Olympics.

There were many small mosquitoes in the house from the open doors in the front and back of the house. Sunday morning I had mosquito bites on both legs, on my knees and on my thighs. There were four bites on the back of my right elbow. I sprayed my pant legs and the floor of my bedroom.

The phone rang, and nobody was up to answer. The teacher got up at 9:30 a.m. and started the laundry. By noon the sun was shining brightly, then a cloudburst of rain moved in, and it rained on and off all afternoon. At 4 p.m. one of the teacher's Bible friends brought in food for dinner, including a carrot cake still warm from baking. That evening I stayed in the living room watching TV until going to bed. Mosquitoes were a problem again. I needed a fan in my bedroom to help keep the mosquitoes away while I slept.

Monday morning a rooster's crow awakened me and I knew that meant there was sunshine. I walked to the HighGate Doll and Craft Factory. The kitchen coordinator came just before noon with pots, baking sheets, cutting boards and graters. The three kitchen helpers removed the labels and washed them. The coconuts that were supposed to be there did not arrive. I worked on the computer. It poured rain in the afternoon and when it stopped, the kitchen helpers went home. The manager of the factory left at 2:30 p.m. to take her twin sons home as they were having problems. I left the factory at the end of the working day to walk the distance to the teacher's home.

The next morning, when I had walked half way to HighGate Doll and Craft Factory, the manager of the factory came along driving in a car and stopped and gave me a ride the remainder of the way. Forty-nine coconuts were delivered to the kitchen that morning though seven were not good. By the time the three kitchen girls removed all the coconut meat from the shells they all had cuts on their hands. Thirty cups of shredded coconut was cooked with twenty-seven cups of brown sugar, salt, and a flask of rum. When there was difficulty cutting some of the finished product, recooking was necessary to make it into rum drops. I walked back to the teacher's home that afternoon.

May 23rd was Jamaica's national Labor Day holiday. HighGate Doll and Craft Factory was closed all day. I spent the day making lace on my travel pillow and watching TV with the teacher and her sons that also had a holiday with nothing else to do that day.

The next morning the wife of the director of the nearby Quaker Friends School came at 8:30 a.m. to move me to their home located on a high hill with a beautiful mountain view. She then drove me to HighGate Doll and Craft Factory, located across the road from the Friends School where she and her husband worked.

That day the production manager arrived at 9:15 a.m., the kitchen manager at 10 a.m., and the first kitchen worker at 11 a.m. The manager of the factory did not come until 1 p.m. I could not get online because of the lack of payment of the factory's bill. That afternoon the three kitchen crew made a batch of lime flavored coconut drops. The baking made the kitchen atmosphere really hot. The workers packaged and labeled the ginger and rum coconut drops they had made earlier.

The wife of the director of the nearby Quaker Friends School came to HighGate Doll and Craft Factory that afternoon with twenty-three students from Oregon's George Fox College to tour the doll and craft factory. I left with them and arrived at the director and his wife's home for 6 p.m. supper. My room in their home was small but clean, with a fan and no mosquitoes. I took the first bath I had since leaving my Oregon home.

The next morning, the director and his wife drove me to HighGate Doll and Craft Factory on their way to the Quaker Friends School for their work. The kitchen manager arrived that morning with her two children that were on school vacation. The kitchen workers husked fifteen coconuts and shredded the meat fine to make Grizzada dough. In the afternoon they cooked a filling for the Grizzada and formed drops and baked them. I used an easel to show the kitchen workers the calculation of costs of the three recipes of coconut drops, and to determine profit from the Jamaican sale price. Some of the coconuts were free so profit was higher for those batches. That day a man from London, representing the European Union, came to meet me and to learn how the kitchen was working that they had built and financed.

Saturday of my second weekend in Jamaica my hosts drove me to Quaker Swift Purcell Home for Boys where a team of nineteen students and two adults from Oregon's George Fox College were having a play day. We joined them at Chapel Service and then went to a HighGate restaurant for dinner. Then we drove to a Girls' Home to practice with the choir for their reunion the following week. We shopped at Port Marie. That evening the director's wife made delicious banana fritters following my idea of how to use her overripe bananas. I helped wash and dry the dishes. We talked until bath and bed time.

A Different World

Sunday of the second week my hosts left at 8:30 a.m. to go with Oregon's George Fox College team to the Blue Mountains. I was shown how to open and close the house locks. Arrangements had been made for a lady to pick me up and take me to HighGate St. Cyprians Anglican Church to a two hour communion service. There were ten hymns, and the sermon ended with a hymn: Hold thou my hand: So weak I am, and helplessness; I dare not take one step without thy aid. Hold thou my hand! O loving Savior, No dread of ill shall make my soul afraid.

That evening the director's wife wanted to watch me making lace so we sat on the front porch and I laced a Buckinghamshire pattern on my travel pillow. That evening we also ate popcorn and coffee cake with a blender papaya drink.

My last week in Jamaica, I rode with the director and his wife every morning to HighGate Dolls and Crafts Factory. There was not much going on that Monday when only the production manager arrived at 11 a.m. and left again at 1 p.m. There was no water in the factory and one of the kitchen girls went to the Quaker Friends School and carried four pails of water to the HighGate Dolls and Crafts Factory kitchen. Then they went shopping for groceries. All three kitchen girls began opening coconuts and cut their hands. They shredded the coconut and made Gizzada dough to finish the filling they made a week earlier, but they could not find whipping cream for coconut macaroons so I changed the recipe.

The Jamaica project.

The Quaker Friends School director and his wife picked me up at the end of the day to return to their home. We ate Jamaican jerk chicken with rice and callaloo that is spinach made with coconut milk and with squash for supper.

Tuesday morning I organized my briefcase before arrival at HighGate Dolls and Craft Factory. The production manager arrived with enough fabric to make a blouse for me and a shirt for my husband. The kitchen workers stayed late on Monday packaging and labeling Grizzada drops. They also cracked more coconuts and grated them fine for grater cakes and macaroons. That morning the kitchen cook boiled green bananas with mackerel and dumplings for lunch so I could taste green bananas. To me they were tasteless.

That afternoon a St. Mary's Parish agent, similar to a USA county agent, picked me up and we drove the road to Annotto Bay, after forded a river, to get to Port Geo and attend a rural woman's meeting of twelve ladies. We were there two hours, and I spoke to the women and gave them recipes I had from Mozambique that they could use for their upcoming culinary work.

My last days at HighGate Doll and Craft Factory I wrote on my final report, and filled plastic bags with grater cakes that are actually candy-like and an attractive red color. I helped label one hundred and ten grater cakes. More coconuts were cracked and shelled.

I demonstrated the use of a pastry blender to make flaky pastry for Gizzada so the dough would not be hard; that was another of my ways of making a difference in the finished products of the school. At noon the kitchen workers asked me to leave the kitchen, and they prepared a party for me while I was in the production room being fitted for a print blouse of Jamaican scenes.

In the afternoon they held a party honoring me: fruit punch, yellow cake, pinwheel sandwiches of red and green layers of cream cheese, and a plate of watermelon spears with fresh pineapple florets at the base of the spears. It was an attractive lunch for all of us and one of the workers' son. Then they cleaned up the kitchen and went home. The remainder of the afternoon I finished my final report on the factory computer.

My departure morning my hosts transported me to HighGate Doll and Craft Factory on their way to Ocho Rios. I said "goodbye" to all of the factory workers when a driver picked me up to drive to Kingston to the Sandhurst Hotel where I had stayed overnight upon entering the country. The driver said banana trees are not trees, they are plants. He described changes in the Jamaican economy when bauxite was once their biggest export in the world. Mahogany trees of Jamaica made mahogany furniture famous years ago, but there are almost no more mahogany trees on the island. Banana exports are also on decline. Jamaica was once the largest banana exporter in the world. The economy had been on the decline since 1970 and never recovered since socialists came into power.

My taxi pickup time was 4:15 a.m. at the hotel the next morning to fly from Kingston to Miami to Dallas/Fort Worth to Oregon. The Jamaican airline breakfast was akee, their delicious national dish, with salt-fish and fried plantain slices and dumpling, croissant and butter, cantaloupe and fresh pineapple.

A privilege of my international volunteer work, to make a difference in the world, was an invitation to a four-day conference in Washington, D.C. I was requested to give a presentation about one of my projects that made a difference in the world, and I showed slides to illustrate my speech. Another day we visited the U.S. Capitol to observe Congress in session in both the House of Representatives and in the Senate. One day we were given a guided tour of the Smithsonian Museum of American History to see the restoration of the Star Spangled Banner, also a tour of the Washington Monument including going to the top of the obelisk. I went to the Natural History Museum to see the big elephant near the entrance, and the tiger exhibit.

One day we went to our organization office for debriefing and meetings before a lovely reception at the Phoenix Park Hotel Ballroom. I met many volunteers at this four-day session, and made many friends that I heard from for many years. The next morning an escort came to the Capitol Hill Holiday Inn and took me to Oregon Senator Gordon Smith's office, and to an appointment with Oregon Congresswoman Darlene Hooley. That day a "rap-up" session lasted until time to take a limousine full of us to the Dulles International Airport and to my flight to Oregon.

My husband and I had been to every continent except Antarctica so we booked an Antarctica cruise that was amazing and beyond description. We were gone three weeks and it was so fantastically beautiful that it made those days impossible to ever forget. There were many days at sea. We enjoyed our cabin on the side where the sun came in. There were few hours of darkness as we were so far south on the January sailing that the sun goes down and shortly thereafter the sun rises again. The sun was always shining in our room when we went to bed. I recalled that living on the earth is expensive, but it does not include a trip around the sun unless one goes in January to Antarctica. We visited the Falkland Islands, Buenos Aires and Ushuaia, Argentina, Punta Arenas, Chile, and Montevideo, Uruguay on the Antarctica cruise.

In my years on every continent I learned where the world's coldest place is located: The Antarctic Plateau. The world's most populated city is Shanghai, China, and the least populated city in the world is Vatican City. The world's most visited city is London. The country that is the most bicycle-friendly in the world is The Netherlands. I had thirty-six round trips to Europe over the years to attend meetings and international projects, and go to World Lace Congresses. There were many more tourists in Europe everywhere I went in the first decade of the 21st century. In this fast-changing world, there were so many people everywhere I went that it was impossible in some countries to get close enough to really see the sites on the itinerary.

Two years, at the request of the Masonic Al Kader Shrine Potentate's Lady, I was guest speaker to present a program for the women while the men were in their monthly business meeting. In an Al Kader publication issue: "I've invited Margaret Palen to our May Stated Meeting to share her incredible handwoven laces and the amazing stories of her work to make a difference in the countries of the world. Lady Shirley invited Margaret during her year and we all thought it was so interesting that we wanted her to come again and share more of her life. I highly encourage you to invite your lady friends and family to join us. It will be an evening they won't forget." In another issue of Al Kader's publication she wrote, "I want to send a very special thank you to Margaret Palen for attending the last Stated Meeting and sharing her incredible talent and experiences. A heartfelt thanks to Margaret Palen for another enjoyable and fascinating presentation for our ladies." It was the third time over many years that I presented a program for the women of Al Kader Shrine that included the world in change as I learned about it in my international projects.

CHAPTER 18
Epilogue

As I grow older, I realize I have lived in the best place in this changing world at the best time in human history. I have learned that knowledge causes one to grow in many directions. I often recall my blessings—a happy memory never wears out.

I marvel at all the changes in the world in my lifetime. I especially like all the modern conveniences that aid my everyday living: air conditioning, dishwashers, microwave ovens, automatic laundry equipment, computers, large TV screens, iPhones, heat pumps, and garage door openers to name a few.

Many countries of the world have marvelous scenery, interesting histories, customs and traditions and people, but every time I stand before the passport officer at the airport I get the urge to kiss my home ground; I'm so thankful for my European ancestors who immigrated to the United States of America.

Most of my good fortune is due to God's blessings, and some of it is courtesy of our founding fathers who based our republic on God's principles. The preservation of religion is totally dependent upon each new generation picking up the baton from the previous generation and carrying it to where it can be passed on to another generation.

Now I look back in time—my drawers, shelves, closets, cabinets, and trunks are full of letters, saved materials covering more than half a century. There are photographs of faces, some with names on the back; others without, silently keeping their secret. There are objects—souvenirs that meant something to me, and gifts. Happily I know their meaning and remember.

These pages are written to relate how it is possible for an American to make a difference in the world.

Margaret recording projects.

www.ingramcontent.com/pod-product-compliance
Lightning Source LLC
Chambersburg PA
CBHW070311230426
43663CB00011B/2081